CATS IN THE BELFRY

Doreen Tovey

summersdale

CATS IN THE BELFRY

Elek Books edition published 1957
(reprinted eight times)
Bantam Books edition published 1993

This edition published in 2005 by Summersdale Publishers Ltd

Reprinted 2005

Summersdale Publishers Ltd
46 West Street
Chichester
PO19 1RP

www.summersdale.com

Printed and bound in Great Britain.

1 84024 452 6

Also by Doreen Tovey:

CONTENTS

ONE

Can She Catch Mice?

Our first Siamese was called Sugieh and we bought her because we had mice. The only excuse I can offer for such Philistine conduct is that they were not ordinary mice. They were the hangers-on of a pet squirrel we had, called Blondin, and over the years they had developed personalities as distinct from ordinary mice as Blondin was different from ordinary squirrels. As different, in fact, as Siamese are from ordinary cats.

During Blondin's lifetime the mice hadn't worried us overmuch. They were always there. Upstairs, downstairs and trekking to and from the wired-in run in the garden where, as the result of an unfortunate *faux pas* when he chewed a hole through the bottom of the sitting room door one day while we were out, to get an apple, Blondin lived during the daytime.

But they were there on business, industriously tracking down the nuts and slices of bread which he was for ever stuffing under carpets and down the sides of chairs against a rainy day. And though it was a little disconcerting the first time I passed one on the landing, pattering along with a nut in its mouth like a dog carrying a bone, in the end I got quite used to them.

There was one who used to play deliberate hide-and-seek with me in the garden house. Eventually he became so tame that at the end of the game he would come out into the open, sit up on his haunches with a piece of bread sticking rakishly out of the corner of his mouth, and look up at me with the expression of an American millionaire wondering how much to offer for Cleopatra's Needle.

There was another one who, finding it impossible to squeeze out between the kitchen door and the outside doorstep one night with a nut in his mouth, left the nut under the door, nipped outside, and ingeniously started trying to hook it up by lying on the doorstep and fishing down through the gap with his paw.

I was scared stiff at the time. All I could see from inside the room was a nut jigging frantically up and down under the door, apparently of its own accord. Blondin, I knew, had nothing to do with it. He was in bed. During the long winter evenings he turned in early, scampering off upstairs to the wardrobe where he slept on a shelf, snoring small but audible snores, inside a pile of Charles's socks. I was so relieved when I spotted the fragile paw of a field mouse groping through the crack and realized that we weren't being invaded by poltergeists that I opened the door and put the nut outside. There was nobody there then, of course – but when I looked out again a few minutes later the nut had vanished.

Had things continued in this friendly vein I might have been writing a book about mice now, instead of Siamese cats. But one wet autumn Blondin caught a chill and died, and within a very short time we were in serious trouble. When the mice found there were no more nuts waiting for them down the sides of the chairs they started chewing holes in the loose covers. When they realized there were none hidden under the carpets they got mad and bit pieces out of those, too. They raided the budgerigar's cage for birdseed and frightened him practically into hysterics – he never had been a very strong bird anyway and was always moulting his tail feathers, and now they were falling out like autumn leaves.

They got into a dresser drawer they had never bothered with in the days of plenty and maliciously chewed all the corners off a big folded damask tablecloth that we only used on special occasions. The next time I opened it, there it was riddled with a pattern of stars and crescents like a Turkish flag and completely unusable. I could almost hear those mice sniggering their silly heads off – and that very night one of them, probably chosen by ballot, ambled airily up the eiderdown and over my face as I lay in bed, just to show me.

The last straw came a few mornings later when I opened the bread-bin and discovered a very small field mouse frantically practising high jumps inside it. He must have sneaked in there for a quiet snack, got himself trapped when the lid was put on, and then completely lost his head. He had been trying for so long to get out by means of those tremendous panic-stricken leaps that they had become mechanical, and when I tipped him out on to the floor he covered the first few yards to the back door jumping like a kangaroo until he suddenly realized that he was free and shot out through the door like a rocket.

That was the end. We had already tried to replace Blondin with another squirrel, and had we been able to do so the balance between mouse and man might have been restored. Blondin himself we had found as a baby, lying injured under a tree, and we had never thought of him as a particularly unusual pet. Now however, as we trudged the town pet shops, enquiring above a murderous cacophony of yelping puppies, mewing kittens, screeching parrots and glugging goldfish for a simple, ordinary little squirrel, it was obvious that the proprietors thought we were mad. Only the Regent's Park Zoo took us seriously – and they, in reply to our anguished pleading, informed us that they had a waiting list for squirrels.

The only thing to do, as we abhorred setting traps for any animal, was to get a cat and hope that after one or two short, sharp executions the mice would take the hint and go away. The trouble was, we weren't particularly keen on cats. We were afraid that if we had one it would attack the birds around the place, some of whom had already become quite tame. In any case, we said, where would we find a cat with the amusing little habits with which Blondin had endeared himself to us – things like biting through the case of Charles's watch to get at the tick, and chewing the corners off our library books or the buttons off people's trousers when they came to tea?

We hesitated, and did nothing. And then, one fateful Sunday morning, we were introduced to Mimi, a young Siamese queen who had recently come to live with the people down the lane. She was six months old and had been given to them by a woman who had gone abroad and been forced to leave her behind. She had been with them for just two weeks, and already the effect on that unimaginative farm labourer's household, where the dog slept outside chained to a draughty kennel and the ordinary cats, kept to catch rats in the outhouses, were never allowed indoors at all, was revolutionary.

Mimi slept not only indoors, but in Father Adams's armchair, on his corduroy waistcoat which he took off specially for her each night before he went to bed. She was never allowed out after dark or when it rained – neighbours spoke in scandalized tones of seeing the old man himself tenderly filling an unmistakable earth-box in the garden after supper.

And now, in this hill village where men prided themselves on their toughness – within living memory they had held kicking matches on the Green and even now you would never catch one of them pushing a pram in his right mind, not even up a hill – here he was, the oldest, toughest, of the lot, parading down the lane as proud as a peacock with a Siamese cat in a harness of bright red rug wool.

He apologized for the harness. Mother, he said, was going to buy her a proper 'un with a bell next time she went to town. Meantime they had to use the wool because Mimi (he pronounced it My-My and it wasn't till months later, when I was helping him make out the pedigrees for her first kittens, that I discovered her original owner had named her after *La Bohème*), Mimi was in season for the first time, and had to be kept away from other cats.

I stared at her in amazement. I had always heard that Siamese queens in that condition nearly drove their owners off their heads yelling and screaming for a husband, and here was one standing in the road as quiet and demure as a nun, with nothing but a strand of rug wool between her and a countryside alive with ranting farmyard toms.

I asked if she *had* a voice. Not half, she said proudly. Bellowed like a ruddy bull when she wanted food, or for him to get out of her chair. But not for a tom. Class, she was. She wouldn't so much as look at an ordinary cat. The harness was only so that he could pick her up quick if a tom attacked her.

Class she certainly was, from her tapered black head, beautiful as an Egyptian queen carved out of ebony, to the tip of her elegant whip tail. I thought she was the loveliest animal I had ever seen, and when the old man went on to tell us how she climbed the curtains like a monkey when the fit took her, perched on the rail, and refused to come down, or went round the room leaping from the top of the piano to the mantelpiece like a racehorse, I knew I was lost. Here was Blondin all over again – with the added advantage, according to the old man, that Siamese cats never broke a thing.

There was just one thing more I wanted to know. Could she, I asked, catch mice? It was like asking a speed maniac if his car could do fifty on the flat. 'Mice,' roared Father Adams in a voice that vibrated with scorn. 'She brut a gert snake in t'other day four foot long, with his 'ead bit clean off, and played with 'un like he were a bit o' string.'

Within a few weeks both Adams and I were sadder, wiser people. The next time she came in season Mimi ripped the seat clean out of the armchair, drove the whole village nearly round the bend with her bawling and finally jumped out of the bedroom window and fled up the lane to the farm, where she was only saved from a fate worse than death by the fact that her dusky Oriental face and blazing blue eyes frightened the battle-scarred old tom who lived there nearly out of his wits, and he was still hiding behind the water-butt when Mrs Adams, wailing and wringing her hands, panted up the hill in her wake.

It was a shaken Father Adams who came down to see us the following Sunday with Mimi, once more quiet and demure, padding sleekly at his heels. He said his wife had got a book about cats out of the library last time she was in town, and according to that Siamese queens couldn't be mated till they were a twelve-month old. If they had to put up with this caper for another six months, he said, with the blasted cat shouting her head off for a tom every few weeks and people knocking on the door and complaining about the noise, it would drive him clean up the pole.

We knew how he felt. We had troubles of our own. Since we saw him last we had acquired Sugieh, and the first thing she had done on entering her new domain was to race up the curtains just like he said, hurl herself like a minute, jet-propelled bomb at the birdcage, and frighten Shorty out of his last remaining tail feather.

She'd had no effect at all on the mice. Only the night before they had chewed a hole in the bag of the vacuum cleaner and when I switched it on a couple of pounds of dirt had gushed out all over our new cream Indian carpet. I was still wondering how I was going to get it up.

TWO

Caesar's Daughter

Sugieh fell in love with us the moment she saw us. It was most embarrassing because we had made up our minds to have a Seal Point like Mimi, and when the breeder said all the Seal Point kittens had gone but perhaps we would like to see the two Blue Points that were left it was understood that we did so merely out of interest.

Unfortunately nobody had told Sugieh that. Her brother, who was as good as sold to a woman who had already bought one of the Seal Points and was coming back for him later if her husband agreed, took one look at us when we went in, strolled off into a corner and started to chew the wireless flex. Sugieh, however, was quite certain we had come for her. She sat there on the hearthrug like a small girl with her suitcase packed ready to go on holiday – her

14

eyes screwed tight with anticipation, her paws pounding up and down like little pistons. When I got down on my knees and spoke to her she opened her eyes for a moment – blue as periwinkles they were, and completely crossed with excitement – greeted us with a squawk that was astounding, considering her size, and screwed them up tight again, waiting for the treat.

Her owner asked if we were intending to breed Siamese ourselves and when we said we were she remarked – just by way of interest, of course – that Sugieh's blue blood was only on her mother's side. Her father was a pure Seal Point, and if she in turn was mated to a pure Seal Point when she grew up, her kittens would be Seal Points as well. Though of course, she said, Blue Points were becoming very popular. Some people thought they had gentler dispositions than the Seal Points, and they were very beautiful. Which reminded her – before we went we really must see Anna.

She opened the door and shouted for Anna at the top of her voice. There was an answering bellow from some distant part of the house, and after a sufficient interval had elapsed for a dignified, unhurried descent of the stairs, Anna appeared.

A Siamese that has apparently just had a blue rinse is, at first sight, something of a shock, and this one reminded me irresistibly of a film star who had married into the aristocracy and gone on from there in a big way. Her legs were long and slender as a gazelle's. Her eyes, which were lighter than those of a Seal Point, glittered like jewelled almonds. She walked as if she owned the earth. If the breeder had reckoned that the sight of Anna would help to sell us Sugieh she was right – but not on account of her beauty. It was the expression of complete hauteur, once she had looked us over, with which that cat swept past us and over to the corner to kiss her son, who was going to a home where they could afford two Siamese.

Not for anything, after that, could we leave Sugieh to be looked down on as the Cinderella of the litter. When we left she went with us, accompanied by a supply of yeast tablets, a bag of minced rabbit and a pedigree bigger than herself which said her father's name was Caesar. That, incidentally, was why we named her Sugieh. We had intended to call her Scheherazade but – though Anna didn't really *marry* the King of Siam – we decided not to complicate history any more than it was already.

Sugieh herself was so happy that that night, for the first and only time in her life, she rode home in the car without a murmur. She ate her supper down to the last crumb. Even the attack on Shorty was only to show us how in future she was going to defend us against All Creatures, great and small. She loved us so much that when at last we went to bed, shutting her in the spare room for Shorty's sake with a hot water bottle and a brand new cat basket to herself, she was heartbroken at the separation. She wailed and screamed and howled, shouting that she was all alone and wanted her mother. She got down and cried under the door so that we could hear her better, and dragged in the end of the rug off the landing, ripping at it in a frenzy that would have done credit to Lady Macbeth. When at last it seemed that there was to be no reprieve she gave a final tragic 'Mow-wow-wow' which trailed sadly off into the darkness. Then there was silence.

Immediately we began to worry. Supposing she lay by the door all night and caught a chill? Father Adams said

Siamese cats died if they caught a chill. Supposing she was dead already? That silence, after the bedlam of the past half hour, was horribly unnatural. We didn't approve of cats sleeping in the bedroom, and we weren't going to start now. All the same… supposing…

Charles was the first to break down. After ten minutes frantically straining his ears to hear some sound from the next room he got sheepishly out of bed muttering that, after all, we had a lot of money tied up in that cat. When we opened the spare room door she was curled up in her basket, having apparently fallen asleep from exhaustion – though it struck me that there was a decided smirk on her face. Charles, being a man, didn't see that. He saw, as he was meant to, only that she looked small and pathetic lying there in the basket, and said – as he was supposed to – that perhaps, for the first night at any rate, we ought to have her in with us. Tenderly he carried her in and deposited her in the crook of my arm where, with a happy sigh, she fell asleep again at once. Charles, with a clear conscience, flopped into his own side of the bed, pulled the clothes over his head and went to sleep himself. Only I stayed awake. I stayed awake because all night long, dreaming nostalgically of Anna, she kept smacking her lips hungrily and loudly right in my ear.

We rose next morning to a pouring wet day and another crisis. Sugieh hadn't used her earth-box. The breeder had advised us, as Sugieh wasn't yet used to a garden, to continue using an earth-box until the weather was better, and we had obligingly provided her with our biggest enamel baking dish filled – as the garden was absolutely sodden and Father Adams said Siamese cats got chills from using damp earth-boxes – with a bag of Shorty's sand. We had shown it to her the night before and she had affected not to see it, which was understandable because Siamese cats are very refined and we had only just met. But now it was morning and Sugieh had been with us twelve hours, and still the sand in her box was as untrodden as the Sahara.

All through breakfast Charles and I kept darting out into the hall and dibbling our fingers encouragingly into the sand. Sugieh darted too, and dibbled happily with a small blue paw. But she wouldn't get into the box. When the time came for us to leave for town I was frantic with worry, for we wouldn't be back until evening and by that time, I felt sure, Sugieh would have burst.

When we got home that night the box was still unused and Sugieh was sitting firmly on the floor. Unburst, but obviously reluctant to move. We were half-way through supper, anxiously wondering whether we ought to call the vet, when Charles had his inspiration. Perhaps, he said, she didn't like sand. It was still raining, so we tried her with sawdust. She didn't like that either. In desperation we cast Father Adams's theories to the wind, filled the box with mud straight from the garden, and put that in front of her. The result was miraculous. With one yell Sugieh was in the box and had flooded it to high-water mark. Supper forgotten, Charles dashed out into the rain at top speed, refilled the box, and offered it to her again. There was no false modesty about Sugieh. She leapt into it once more, raised her small spike of a tail and speedily reseated herself, thanking heaven at the top of her voice that we had at last realized Mother had taught her it was Dirty to use anything but Earth.

That was that crisis over. But there were plenty more to follow. There was the first time she went into the garden, for instance. The path was bad enough – she grumbled all the way out that the gravel was hurting her feet – but when we put her down on the lawn and the stubbly grass prickled her paws for the first time she let out one shriek and fled straight up my leg, swearing something had bitten her. She did the same when she saw her first dog, only this time she went on up over my face and stood on my head for extra safety, bawling at him just to try and get her *now*, that was all.

It was most discouraging. Blondin used to do that too, when he was frightened. One old man I know nearly signed the pledge on the spot the night he met me in the lane just after closing time and saw a squirrel yelling defiance at him from the top of my head with his tail bushed out like a flue brush. All the thanks I got, too, for assuring him that it really was a squirrel and not the first sign of d.t.'s, was that he made a gate-to-gate tour of the village telling everybody I was potty. What they would say when they heard I went round now with a screaming cat on my head I shuddered to think.

When Sugieh's feet toughened up and she began to venture outside on her own we had more trouble. The first time she went into the garden unaccompanied she climbed up to the garage roof, slid down the back slope and fell into the water-butt. She got out by herself, stalked into the house stiff-legged with indignation and delivered such a harangue, while green, stagnant water dripped steadily off her tail on to our poor Indian carpet, that Charles slunk out in self-defence and made a cover for the butt on the spot. Unfortunately the next time she went into the bathroom and saw Charles lying in the bath she remembered her own narrow escape, gave one horrified yell, and plunged in to the rescue. Charles had his eyes shut at the time and when Sugieh landed on his stomach screeching like a banshee it frightened him so much he leapt up and nearly stunned himself on the first aid cabinet, which had been fixed over the bath in the first place to keep it out of Blondin's reach.

After that Sugieh fell into the bath so often trying to save us from drowning that we had to tie a notice to the taps reminding us to lock the door before we turned them on. Then – presumably to counteract the effect of getting wet so much – she took to standing, when she talked to us, with her rear bang up against the electric fire. Twice she caught the tip of her tail alight, though she was so busy lecturing us she never noticed it. On each occasion Charles threw himself across the room in a magnificent rugby tackle and put out the flame before it touched her skin, but he said it was bad for his heart at his age, and it wasn't doing mine much good either. In the end we had to buy small-mesh guards that completely spoiled the look of any room they were in, and tie them to every fire in the house with string.

Worst of all was the problem of food. When she lived with Anna, Sugieh had, it seemed, eaten her prescribed two cereal meals, two meat meals and four yeast tablets a day with meek obedience. But not with us. As from the second day, by which time she had summed us up as a couple of suckers and dead easy to handle, she refused to eat any more cereal. When we had liver, which she was supposed to have not more than once a week, or bacon which she wasn't supposed to have at all, she sat on the breakfast table, no matter who else was there, and dribbled like Oliver Twist. On the other hand she ate rabbit – which was good for her and so cheap at that time that the butcher looked pained if I asked for less than a pound – only when the spirit moved her, so that I was for ever tipping dishes of turned-off meat into the lane for the benefit of less fortunate little cats. Needless to say as soon as the less fortunate little cats arrived Sugieh went out, elbowed her way through the crowd and scoffed the rabbit with such gusto that one old lady practically wore a groove in the front path coming in to tell us that our dear little cat was eating scraps in the lane, and did we think perhaps we didn't give her enough to eat?

She condescended to eat a little steak occasionally, but even then it had to be tossed to her piece by piece, and aimed so that it landed directly in front of her. If it dropped so much as an inch beyond her reach she ignored it. If it fell on her fur she ran upstairs and hid under the bed, screaming that we had hit her. If we put down a whole plateful of food at any time she shook her back leg delicately in the gesture she used to indicate she had finished with her earth-box and walked away with her ears sleeked back in horror at our grossness.

She liked milk, but only if she was allowed to drink it standing on the table, out of a jug. We got over that by keeping her milk in the jug and filling our own cups surreptitiously, so as not to offend her, from the bottle, which we kept behind the bookcase. People said we were foolish, and we ought to make her drink out of a saucer. They didn't know Sugieh. She was the living example of an iron hand in a small, blue-pointed glove. The only thing she would drink out of a saucer was coffee – and that was only because the coffee cups were too small for her to get her head in.

As for her yeast tablets – obviously Anna had indelibly impressed on her the importance of eating those regularly if she wanted to grow up a big strong cat and keep human beings in their place, but she ate them in such a revolting manner, with her face screwed up and her mouth open, dropping half-chewed tablets on to the carpet and then licking them up again, each time more soggy and repulsive-looking than the last, that we just dumped four of those in front of her every night and bolted into the kitchen, so that we wouldn't have to watch.

THREE

Help! Kidnapped!

When I went home one evening after Sugieh had been with us for about a month and announced that my firm wanted me to go to Liverpool on business and it would mean my being away overnight, Charles looked at me in horror. Who, he asked, was going to look after the cat?

He was, I said brightly. There was nothing to it. Just give her shredded rabbit for supper, making sure there weren't any bones in it; fish for breakfast – be very careful about the bones in that and be sure it didn't boil over on the stove; change her earth-box night and morning – if she yelled at him with an urgent expression on her face it meant it wanted changing in between as well; wipe her if she got wet; see that she didn't play with Mimi, who had designs on being the only Siamese in the district and was inclined to try and murder Sugieh if nobody was looking; make sure she had her yeast tablets and didn't stay out after dark; see that she didn't –

At that moment there was a loud splash, followed by a wail. Sugieh, who had been looking for fresh fields to conquer ever since she was barred from the bathroom, had fallen down the lavatory. She couldn't have chosen a worse time to do it. If I had, even for a few brief seconds, hoped that Charles would agree to looking after her, that moment was now past. He took one look at her as I hauled her squirming and yelling from the depths, shuddered, and said he had just had an idea. We would ask my grandmother to have her for the night, then he could drive me up to Liverpool by car and we could both have a rest.

My grandmother loved animals and had, fortunately, not encountered Sugieh to date, so we had no difficulty in fixing that up. What we hadn't bargained for was that since that first journey out from town, when she sat sedately on my lap watching the traffic with wide-eyed interest and occasionally – hypocrite that she was – smirking affectionately up into my face, Sugieh had developed a Thing about cars.

The moment I got into the car with her the morning of that ill-fated trip, before Charles had even so much as pressed the starter, she began to yell: Charles patted her on the head as she sat on my lap and told her not to be a silly girl, she knew she liked carsy-warsies. With Sugieh, of course, that was just asking for trouble. By the time we got to the top of the hill leading to the main road she was standing on her hind legs, clawing frantically at the window and shrieking for help. Charles said it was the noise of the bottom gear upsetting her; once we got on the flat road she'd be all right. I have no doubt at all that Sugieh understood every word we said, because by the time we were half-way to town and the road had been flat as a pancake for miles all the other drivers were gesturing violently at us as they passed, threatening to punch Charles's nose for swerving all over the place and not giving signals, and Charles himself was shouting that if I didn't get that damblasted cat off his neck she'd have us up a telegraph pole.

It was even worse on the return trip. First of all we had my aunt to contend with. My grandmother's concern for animal welfare had always gone to extremes. When she was younger she had had a tame owl called Gladstone whose favourite perch was on top of the bathroom door. My father swore that sometimes it was so draughty with the door open you could see waves on the bath water and in the winter my grandfather used ostentatiously to bring a hip bath down from the attic and wash in his bedroom instead, but it made no difference. Grandma wouldn't have the door shut. She took the line that human beings could look after themselves but poor dumb animals couldn't, so you either took your bath with Gladstone glaring ghoulishly down at you – as like as not with a piece of dead mouse lovingly provided by Grandma in his claws – or not at all.

I can remember her myself hurrying down, armed with my old push-chair and scarlet with indignation, to fetch home a collie which somebody told her had been pledged at the local pawnshop. Actually the pawnbroker had taken the dog in, without any hope that the owner would ever redeem it, rather than see it starve; and he had looked after it quite well. Nothing would convince my grandmother, however, that it hadn't been heartlessly ticketed and stacked with the rest of the goods in pawn. She wheeled it home in the push-chair telling everybody she met that it couldn't walk and reducing them practically to tears with the harrowing story – quite untrue – of how she had lifted it off the pawnshop shelf with her Own Two Hands. I remember it so well because for a fortnight after that I was the one deputed to push Baldwin, as she called him – this of course was years after Gladstone had eaten his last mouse on top of the bathroom door – to the park in the pram every day for an airing. And when at last Grandma decided he was strong enough to stand on his own feet again, I was the one – Grandma said she knew I loved poor dumb animals just as much as she did and God would reward me for it – who was persuaded to take him for his first walk and, in consequence, had to face the music when he promptly jumped into the first pram he came to and sat on the baby.

She was just as firm in her convictions even when, in later years, she grew too old actually to look after the animals herself. The first time we left Blondin with her, for instance, in spite of our assurances that he would be perfectly happy locked in the spare room with his basket and climbing branches she insisted that my Aunt Louisa had him in her bedroom in case he was lonely.

If he had been locked in the spare room Blondin would have settled down quite happily in the wastepaper basket filled with old pullovers which he used in the garden house, but when he saw my aunt's comfortable bed it proved too much for him. He grabbed a nut, dived under the eiderdown, and there he stayed all night, rattling his teeth like castanets every time the poor soul moved.

She complained about it the next day but my grandmother merely asked sternly whether she was man or mouse, to be afraid of an innocent little creature who had come to her for comfort. After fifty years of living with Grandma poor Aunt Louisa was, alas, indubitably mouse, so for the next fortnight she shared her bed with Blondin and his nuts, hardly slept a wink, and discovered on the last morning that, tired of sleeping *under* the eiderdown, which presumably allowed draughts to seep in through the gaps, Blondin had chewed a hole in the cover and was blissfully asleep inside. My Grandma was furious about that, I remember, but not with Blondin. With my aunt who, she said, shouldn't have allowed him to do it.

It was a foregone conclusion of course that if we left Sugieh with them Grandma would make my aunt take her to bed too, but we didn't see much harm in that. Sugieh, despite our original resolutions, often slept with us. Within a week of her arrival she had worked out that if she nipped smartly upstairs when she heard the hot water bottles being filled and hid under the dead centre of the bed we couldn't get her out. Then, when the room was in darkness and she judged we had had time to go to sleep, she would creep out, climb on to the bed and insert herself so gently under the bedclothes and into my arms that I hadn't the heart to move her.

Apart from snoring, the only disturbance she caused us was when, promptly at five in the morning, she got up and stropped her claws on the padded top of the blanket box, but as my aunt didn't have a blanket box we thought there was nothing to worry about. How were we to know that

Sugieh would choose her visit to develop a Thing about woollen clothes?

We learned later that among other dark, Oriental aspects of their nature which only come to light when they have firmly established themselves in some soft-hearted household, Siamese are often confirmed wool-eaters. A breeder who is something of a cat psychologist told us that he believes they do it to comfort themselves when they are lonely, in the same way that children suck their thumbs, and it is a fact that our present cats, having each other for company, never eat wool except when travelling. We put them in separate baskets then and Solomon, Sugieh's big, burly son, invariably drags the end of the car rug in through the wickerwork and chews it steadily, between muffled sobs, all the way to his destination.

My aunt, however, was no psychologist. When she went up to bed that night and found that Sugieh had eaten several large holes in her bedsocks she just got so plain, unpsychologically mad that she tucked the sheets firmly round her head and refused to let our dear little kitten get in with her. Sugieh, unused to such unfriendly treatment, got so mad in turn that when Aunt Louisa, who always wore wool next to her skin, woke up in the morning, she found holes in everything she had taken off overnight as well. She got no sympathy from my grandmother, who laughed her head off when she heard about it – and Sugieh, locked in the spare room to prevent further damage, spent the day swearing horrible oaths at the top other voice and leering under the door at my Grandma's fat black neuter, who sat transfixed with horror on the other side. That upset my aunt too. She worried so much in case the two cats got at each other and had a fight that by the time we arrived, late in the evening, she was practically hysterical with suppressed guilt because she had been too scared to open the door and give Sugieh any food and too scared, afterwards, to confess it to my grandmother.

We drove home in silence, shaken by the impact of one small Siamese kitten on that tranquil Victorian household, while in the back seat Sugieh continued happily with her game of Kidnapped. This time, while there was nobody else about, she sat there quite quietly, bolt upright with her paws together, her tail tucked primly round them, and the expression on her face of a dowager duchess returning from the theatre. The moment she saw lights, however, whether in a house or a passing car, she flew to the window, pressed herself pathetically against it and screamed wildly for help. She staged a magnificent performance going past a cinema just when the late-night audience was coming out, beating her paws against the window with a frail, pathetic frenzy that would have done credit to Lilian Gish. But where she really excelled herself was when we drew up at the traffic lights at the busy town centre. Most Siamese sound uncannily like human babies when they cry, but Sugieh that night outdid any Siamese or human baby I have ever known. She sobbed, she wailed, she howled, until people on the pavement began peering into the car with set faces looking for the little orphan who was apparently being simultaneously beaten, starved and tortured inside. By that time, needless to say, Sugieh was out of sight, doing her ventriloquist act from under Charles's seat. The only thing that saved us from being mobbed by a crowd of angry passers-by was the last-minute changing of the lights and the fact that Charles, having been something of a racing driver in his gilded youth, was away off the mark like a shot.

We never took Sugieh to my grandmother's again. Charles's nerves wouldn't stand it. The next time we went on holiday we arranged to leave her with a family from the next village who fell in love with her one day when they walked past and saw her playing innocently in the garden and pleaded that if at any time we wanted to go away we would send her to stay with their own Siamese, James.

We accepted with alacrity. At the last moment our consciences did get the better of us and we rang up explaining that it wasn't really fair to expect anybody outside a lunatic asylum to take our cat and we'd better call the whole thing off, but our new friends wouldn't hear of it. James, they said, who had been a real cat-about-town until the age of three, when he underwent an operation that had become imperative if they were to continue to share the same house with him, had turned so sanctimonious in recent months that they felt somebody like Sugieh about the place might do him good.

She did too. The only peace the Smiths got that fortnight was during the evenings, when she and James sat in solemn consultation inside a gramophone console whose works had gone for repair. When the lid was lifted two heads would appear through the turntable hole – one Roman-nosed, dark and aristocratically handsome; the other small, blue and slightly cross-eyed – gaze reprovingly upon the intruder and vanish again into the depths. There, it seemed, they planned the mischief for the following day, which began with a free-for-all steeplechase at five a.m. – Sugieh's idea that; James never got up till mid-day in the normal way – and continued in crescendo until supper-time when they appeared, sleek, well-mannered, hair metaphorically parted in the middle, ate their meal with regal dignity and disappeared once more inside the gramophone.

In between they played plain bedlam. We had forgotten to warn the Smiths about Sugieh's addiction to water and she dived into the fishpond three times, followed by the obedient James, before they realized it was no accident and covered it with wire netting, while it took the whole family plus the postman to rescue James from the top of a fifty-foot fir tree where Sugieh had enticed him and then, Delilah-like, left him clinging terror-stricken while she skipped lightly down and taunted him from the lawn.

James thought himself no end of a dog when he was safely down though. He stalked around stiff-legged as an Arab, looking up at the tree and bellowing at everybody to see where *he'd* been, while Sugieh gazed at him with soft, big-eyed admiration. In return he stole one of Mrs Smith's fur gloves for Sugieh to play with, and taught her to dig holes in the garden.

A great step forward, that was. We had been trying for a long time to get Sugieh to dig in the garden instead of using an earth-box, but to no avail. Now, with her friend James to guide her, she suddenly caught on. Not, mind you, to what the holes were for; she would break off and rush indoors to her earth-box for that. Just that cats dug holes. For the remainder of the fortnight she and James dug holes so industriously all over the Smith's garden that by the time we came back from holiday the place looked like a battlefield.

The Smiths didn't mind, though. They were very long-suffering. As they said, people who keep Siamese have to be if they don't want to go mad.

FOUR

Trouble in the Valley

That summer our quiet country village resounded to a host of noises it had never known before; the loudest and most consistent of which were the shrieks of startled pheasants running for their lives and the clatter as the bottom fell out of Shorty's cage.

Why Sugieh had to chase pheasants when we lived practically next door to the gamekeeper we never knew, but it was typical of her. Anything for a sensation. She only had to hear the slightest rustle in the copse across the road and she was off like a shot, regardless of who might see her.

Once it happened when the Rector was with us in the garden, holding, with the Harvest Festival in view, a leisurely conversation about marrows. One moment Sugieh was sitting modestly at his side doing her best to look like a

Sunday School teacher and the next all you could see of her was a small white rear disappearing battlewards into the undergrowth, fifty yards away.

Fortunately the Rector was short-sighted and a little deaf and so missed the alarming spectacle a few seconds later, when a dozen pheasants erupted precipitately out of a gorse patch and fled up the hill with Sugieh, hard behind them, whooping like a Red Indian. Even more fortunately he had gone home again before she returned and missed hearing what Charles called her when she came back pheasant-less, marched straight indoors and knocked Shorty off his hook.

People have different ways of working off temper. Small boys kick walls. Charles used to slam doors – until Blondin narrowly escaped becoming a Manx squirrel one morning when Charles was particularly mad with the Government. After that, since having to look both sides of a door *and* on top before slamming it rather spoilt the effect, he took up smoking. Sugieh's remedy for all *her* frustrations, from falling out of a tree through too much showing off to being clouted by Mimi for being cheeky, was to knock down Shorty.

We got wise to her in the end. When we saw her stumping down the path with her ears flat and her tail stiff as a starched poker we used to nip in and lock Shorty in the bathroom. Sometimes, however, we weren't on the spot when she got frustrated, and the first we knew about it was the crash, mingled with the frantic ringing of the budgie bell, as the cage came off its stand.

She never hurt Shorty. After the first couple of crashes Charles worked out mathematically where the cage would land and we kept an armchair permanently on the spot. But Shorty used to get awfully mad about it. When we rushed in to the rescue they were always in the same position. Sugieh on the arm of the chair with her nose against the bars, shouting all the things she dared not call Mimi, and Shorty – keeping carefully to the middle of the cage – bouncing up and down with rage and screaming back like a Hyde Park heckler.

The only damage she did, other than to our nerves, was to knock the cage so out of shape that eventually the bottom came off and had to be tied on, like the fire-guards, with string. It still fell off every time she hit the cage, but as the cage always landed right way up in the armchair Shorty came to no harm and always thoroughly enjoyed the sequel in which Sugieh, screaming wildly for Anna and the RSPCA, got her bottom smacked on the spot.

It wasn't, we discovered as the months went by, that Sugieh was particularly wicked. It was just that she was a Siamese. After a while we found we could recognize fellow Siamese owners almost at sight by their harassed expressions and the way they flinched at unexpected noises. All of them had hair-raising tales to tell of their experiences. There was Ho, for instance, who lived at the other end of the village and whose ambition seemed to be to get himself jailed for felony, with his mistress as an accessory after the fact. Ho just walked into other people's houses, stole anything he thought his owner would like, and took it home to her. His mistress, who was a pillar of the WI and terribly worried about the whole thing, spent anguished hours restoring to the rightful owners love-gifts which ranged from a pair of unwashed socks to a Victoria sandwich still in its box. Even she, however, was floored the time he came back with a brand new skein of yellow wool which nobody claimed and followed it up next morning with a complete knitted sleeve in the same colour. The mystery was only solved when on the third day he came in with the rest of the knitting still on the needles, and by following the trailing wool through two hedges, round a pond and up a lane (like all criminals he had made his one mistake and left the ball behind) she traced it back to a farmer whose wife was away for the weekend and hadn't missed it.

There was Basil, who – hag-ridden perhaps by his unfortunate name – went upstairs whenever visitors came and brought down the bath sponge. That may sound harmless enough, but the sight of a cat in a strange house eternally slinking round behind a bath sponge can be quite unnerving. At least two visitors, unused to the ways of Siamese, never went there again.

There was Heini, who persistently stole the golliwog belonging to the little girl next door even after his mistress bought him an identical one of his own. Heini, too, was so attached to a stair carpet which he had turned, after months of hard work, from Wilton into a remarkable imitation of Astrakhan that when his owner had the house converted into two flats, with her own new front door at the top of the stairs, he howled himself into a decline for two days until she had the door rebuilt at the bottom so that he could be with his beloved carpet.

There was – but why go on? Compared with other people's cats Sugieh was as innocent as a Botticelli angel; even if she had just swatted the heads off all the tulips in mistake for butterflies.

Charles said her trouble was surplus energy, and if we took her for walks she might work it off. She did to begin with. The first time we took her out across the hills she was so overcome that she walked three miles through this strange new wonderland with eyes as round as Alice's and never uttered a word. And when she got back she was so tired she fell asleep without even waiting for her supper.

Not for nothing, though, was her father's name Caesar. After a few trips she was the one who led us up the hills with her tail raised like a battle banner, and Charles – who had to rescue her from near-catastrophe practically every time we went out – was the one who sank into an armchair when we got home and reached for the brandy.

Again and again he had to climb trees after her. Not because she couldn't get down by herself, but because she liked being rescued from trees. It made her feel feminine.

Once she chased a fox. True it was a vixen with a cub and the vixen's chief concern, from the moment Sugieh opened her big mouth and shrieked at them to stop, was undoubtedly to get her child away from this terrifying creature with sky-blue eyes and a bray like a donkey's. All the same I died a dozen deaths until Charles hauled Caesar's daughter – safe, but swearing fit to burst – out of the bramble thicket where she had finally lost them.

One dreadful evening, pushing her inquisitive nose through a gap in the mowing grass just off the main track, she flushed a courting couple. The worst part of that affair was that the young man occasionally did odd jobs for us and was a friend of Sugieh's, so instead of crossing her eyes warningly at them and passing on, which was her usual way with strangers, she immediately sat down and began to bawl for us to Come and See who she'd found Here – the Nice Young Man who mended our Cistern. We dragged her away eventually by the scruff of her neck. All of us were scarlet with embarrassment; indeed the young lady, who had hidden her head in her boy friend's lapel and was by this time sobbing with mortification, was so embarrassed that even the back of her neck was red. Sugieh didn't notice it. Slung over Charles's shoulder like a sack of potatoes she continued to shout back greetings long after we had hurried out of sight, and the next time the young man came to work for us she ran up to him and started yattering so excitedly he had no doubt at all as to what she was talking about. He blushed all over again on the spot.

We realized then why people take Siamese cats out on leads. Not to protect the cats, but to protect the public. Next time we went to town we, too, bought a lead and harness for Sugieh.

The result of that was as alarming as it was unexpected. The moment we put Sugieh on a lead she went up and down on the end like a yo-yo, screaming that we were Putting her in Chains, got her back feet securely hooked up round her ears, and threw a fit in the middle of the lawn. Other Siamese owners, glancing smugly at cats who, though they were all psychological cases in other ways, at least sat like slit-eyed Buddhas when they were in harness, told us we must persevere. We did. We persevered so hard we nearly had a fit ourselves at the very thought of taking Sugieh for a walk, but we never got her used to a harness. In the end she did agree, in order that we might hold up our heads among our fellow humans, to wearing a collar attached to the lightest of cords. Not round her neck. That apparently made her feel like a galley slave. Round her middle, where it gave her the appearance of a hula dancer and was, as she and we were perfectly aware, completely useless. The moment she saw anything she wanted to chase she just slipped her back legs out of it and went.

The one thought that sustained us through that long, calamitous summer was that one day Sugieh would grow up and have kittens. There had been a time when we had looked forward to having kittens for their own dear little sakes – and, of course, because if we could sell them for anything like the price we had given for Sugieh we would be able to retire after a couple of litters. Now our only thought was that they might sober her down.

Up the lane Father Adams was fervently hoping the same about Mimi, and meeting with unexpected snags. After Mimi's initial attempt at eloping with the cat from the farmyard Father Adams had taken the strictest precautions to preserve her virtue. The first yell that appeared to his anxious ear to contain a note of passion; the first suggestion of voluptuous rolling on the ground – and Mimi, even if she had only been taking a dust bath, was locked in the attic with her earth-box until all danger was past.

At length, however, to the intense relief of the neighbours, Mimi attained her first birthday and Father Adams started looking round for a suitable mate. His first shock – and it shook him to the core – was the discovery that every Siamese male for miles around had been neutered. His second was the discovery, after riding ten miles on his bike to contact a lady whom he had lauded to the skies before he went because she had, he said, had the decency to leave a cat as nature made it, that she wanted a three guinea stud fee.

He nearly had apoplexy when he heard that. According to his reckoning, while it was perfectly all right for him to sell Mimi's kittens and make money out of them – he had in fact already confided in us that he expected to make more out of her than out of his strawberries that season – for anybody to charge for a tom's services bordered on rank immorality. Nobody, he bellowed when he came back, thumping his fist on our front gate till it rattled – he always did that when he felt strongly about something, and we wished he wouldn't; it looked as if we were the ones he was having the row with – *nobody* but an old maid would have thought of such a thing and he was damned if he'd encourage her.

Heaven knows what would have happened, what with Mimi shrieking her head off with frustrated passion up in the attic and her owner stubbornly refusing either to pay for a pedigree husband or to let her mate, for the sake of peace, with the torn from the farmyard – we explained genetics to him by the hour but we couldn't shake his conviction that if she once Went Wrong, as he delicately put it, she would produce piebald kittens for evermore – if he hadn't, at the crucial moment, changed his doctor.

Father Adams was always changing doctors. He had had two new ones since we knew him. The first he changed because he drove a fast sports car and when the National Health contributions went up Father Adams blamed it directly on his petrol consumption. The second he changed, presumably by way of making a clean sweep, at the same time as his dentist, when he had trouble with his false teeth.

Now he had changed again, to a doctor who had just come to live in a neighbouring village. Father Adams, who signed up with him the day after his arrival, said he was a proper nice young man and understood his arthritis perfectly. It was, we understood, pure coincidence that he had an unneutered Siamese tom named Ajax. It was pure coincidence, too, that the next time Mimi came in season Father Adams had such a chronic attack of arthritis he had to stay in bed and send for the new doctor.

He was an understanding young man. As soon as he heard Mimi screeching in the attic and learned the sad story of her unrequited love he drove straight back home and fetched Ajax. He must have been a good doctor too. That very evening Father Adams's arthritis was so much better he was able to hobble triumphantly down to the Rose and Crown.

FIVE

Trouble Everywhere

Sugieh came into season for the first time in September, while we were in Scotland and she was once more staying with the Smiths. We were afraid she might. According to the book it could happen with a precocious Siamese as early as four months, and as Sugieh was by this time seven months old and so precocious it made you want to spit, it was obvious she was saving her efforts for a special occasion.

With the aid of James she staged it magnificently. She uttered her first call in the middle of a dinner party and scared everybody, including herself, nearly out of their wits. The Smiths, realizing what was happening, had hardly finished assuring the more nervous guests that she was not going mad when she called again, louder than before. Whereupon, they told us, their eyes glazing slightly at the memory, James, hearing her voice through the mists of sleep and forgetting for the moment that he was no longer the cat he had been, had leapt gallantly out of the gramophone and tried to make love to her on the hearthrug, and Sugieh had shinned up the standard lamp in alarm and brought it down in the cutlets.

It said much for the Smiths that, even after that, we still remained friends. They wouldn't even let us pay for the lamp. They did warn us, though, that Sugieh was what they termed an exceptional caller. Eventually they had had to lock her in their spare room, and though James was allowed to visit her whenever he liked and within a couple of days had succeeded in persuading her that there were other things in life besides love – she emerged, they said, as placidly as if it had never happened, drank a jug of milk to cool her throat and went happily off with him to dig holes in the garden – while it lasted they had been quite unable to hear themselves speak.

It was quite a while before we heard her ourselves. After that first effort she went so long without calling again that in fact we began to get suspicious. Those moonlit October nights when she had refused to come in and we had gone to bed without her, lying awake worrying about foxes and badgers until, around midnight, she would come tearing up the stairs bellowing that she hadn't any idea of the time and why on earth hadn't we called her? Had she perhaps gone innocently into the woods and been pounced on, even as she opened her mouth for her first tremulous call, by some feline Don Juan? Or had she – which was much more likely, knowing Sugieh – kept her love pangs to herself and gone deliberately off to look for a tom, realizing from her experience with the Smiths that if she let out one squeal while we were around we would lock her up and spoil all the fun?

Sugieh knew, but she wasn't telling. As the weeks wore on and we eyed her more and more suspiciously – there was no doubt at all that she was getting plumper, though that might have been because she was growing out of kittenhood – all she did was smirk coyly and stretch so that we could get a better look. When we asked her sternly what she had been up to, she half-closed her eyes and gave a faint, ecstatic squawk.

Christmas drew nearer, Sugieh still hadn't called, and eventually there was no doubt at all in our minds. While up the lane Father Adams rubbed his hands and prepared gleefully for Mimi's happy event, we shook our heads reproachfully at Sugieh and prepared to conceal her shame.

As it happened we were all wrong. Mimi, to Father Adams's chagrin, had a false pregnancy and produced no kittens at all while Sugieh, tickled pink at the way she had fooled us, came triumphantly into season on Christmas Day, roaring like a lion. It seemed that social occasions had that effect on her. After a feed of turkey – never shall I forget the look of awe on her face when she saw a turkey for the first time; you could see her mentally writing off those pheasants on the spot – a run in the woods to see if there were any more turkeys up there, and a brisk game of snakes and ladders which she won by sweeping all the counters on to the floor, she suddenly threw herself on her back and burst into song. My brother-in-law looked at her in alarm and asked what was wrong. Mindful that there were children present I looked at him meaningly and said Nothing. She got like that sometimes, when she was Excited. Our nine-year-old twin nephews, looking at each other in horror, promptly put aside their snakes and ladders and explained that she was making *that* noise because she wanted a husband.

The Smiths were right about her being an exceptional caller. Sugieh had always had a powerful voice, even for a Siamese, and her love song was excruciating. By day she followed us round the house screaming and throwing herself hopefully on her back every time we looked at her. At night she thumped round in the spare room, yelling more furiously than ever because, unable to stand the racket at such close quarters, we refused to let her come to bed with us. By dawn on the morning after Boxing Day we could stand it no longer. Charles, loudly damning all Siamese to perdition, took her down and shut her in the bathroom.

Ours is an old place and the bathroom is not only on the ground floor but separated from the original part of the cottage by a two-foot thick stone wall. When after a while the screams, now mercifully faint, stopped altogether we told ourselves smugly that Sugieh was no fool; she knew when we had her beaten. For the first time in two days we prepared to get some sleep.

A split second later the father and mother of all cat fights started up in the garden, and we nearly went through the roof. 'Sugieh!' I screeched, barely touching ground as I leapt out of bed and down the stairs. 'Quick!' urged Charles – stopping nevertheless to put on his slippers and belt his dressing-gown before pelting after me.

Sugieh was quite safe. She had not, as by this time we suspected her of being perfectly capable of doing, gone through the ventilator or prised the window open with a crowbar. She was sitting in the bathroom window like the queen of a medieval tourney, squinting with smug delight while outside two lusty knights battled for her favours in the polyanthus.

She stayed in season for a week and each night, with unfailing regularity, there was a cat fight outside the bathroom window. A fortnight later she began calling again. We had intended waiting until she was a year old before having her mated, but it was more than flesh and blood could stand. At eleven months Sugieh, with great enthusiasm, became a bride.

She was mated – the maiden lady's tom being in our opinion too flat-faced, and Ajax being unromantically laid up with an abscess in his ear – to a cat called Rikki, at a Siamese cattery forty miles away. Rikki's owners said she was one of the most forward cats they had ever seen. She was also, they said, the loudest. Normally it took about four days to make sure that young queens, who were often nervous, were properly mated, but on the evening of the second day they 'phoned to say there was no doubt at all about Sugieh and would we please fetch her as soon as possible because she was disturbing all the other cats while Rikki, far from being the triumphant male, was padding round his enclosure with a haunted look on his face and jumping every time he heard her voice.

At least, we thought, as we drove wearily home that night with Sugieh in the back still sobbing hysterically for her beloved husband – her owners had told us to keep her indoors for a couple of days or, love-him-forever or not, she might console herself with the farmyard tom and still have mongrel kittens – at least after *this* was over we should have some peace.

We were always forecasting things like that about Sugieh, and we were always wrong. After the noisiest marriage in the history of the cattery Sugieh embarked on a pregnancy which couldn't have been more involved if she'd read a doctor's book. First, after two days of dewy-eyed dreaming about Rikki – she couldn't waste any more time than that; she only had nine weeks to get everything in – she developed Morning Sickness. Either that or she was suddenly overcome with shame at the thought of her scandalous behaviour at the cattery. The result was, anyway, that she went completely off her food, sat around looking frail and swaying slightly with closed eyes – and finally, with a temperature of 104, had to be driven dramatically through a snowstorm for streptomycin injections.

No sooner did we get her over that – 'When you love animals they make you their slaves,' said the vet gazing sentimentally into her sad blue eyes, but even he couldn't have anticipated the scene when, suddenly recovering her appetite in the middle of the night, she insisted on being fed with crab paste on Charles's pillow – she developed a passion for jam tarts. They had to be jam tarts, though she never ate the jam; and they had to be stolen. If we gave her one she retched realistically, shook her back leg at it and walked away. Left alone, however, she would clear a plateful in a day, stealing them from the pantry and carrying them off to the bathroom, where she carefully ate the pastry rims and left the middles on the floor and Charles absent-mindedly trod them all over the house.

Fired, we imagined, by a desire that her kittens should all be Seal Points like Rikki – a real Yul Brynner of a cat he had been, with massive black shoulders and a wicked, wedge-shaped head – she also drank more coffee than it seemed possible a cat could hold, and, for some unfathomable reason, took to chewing paper; a habit which, the day she ate Charles's Aunt Ethel's telegram, landed us in serious trouble.

Charles's Aunt Ethel, when she decided to stay with members of the family, always announced her impending arrival by telegram; that way the family had no chance to get out of it. In our case, as we lived, as she was always telling us, at the back of beyond, the telegram also contained the time of the train so that Charles could drive over to the station and collect her.

When, therefore, she appeared dramatically on the doorstep one cold wet night, looking grimly at us over the top of her streaming pince-nez and announcing that not only had she Waited in Vain for a whole hour at the junction but the taxi she had then been Forced to Take had broken down at the end of the lane (it always did for strangers; Fred Ferry had no intention of taxing his springs on our potholes if he could help it), it was obvious that we were for it.

She wouldn't believe we hadn't had the telegram. She had Sent It, she said, and that was that. It didn't help, either, when Charles rang the post office – rather irately, to impress Aunt Ethel – and asked what the devil they'd done with it. The postmaster, who was a man of spirit, said what the devil did we think? Pushed it under the door himself he had, while he was out for a walk, and had his hand grabbed by a blasted cat. Why, he wanted to know, couldn't we have a letter-box, like ordinary normal people?

We did have a letter-box. It was, as the regular postman knew, in the kitchen door. Charles had transferred it from the front door after Blondin nearly decapitated himself one day through sticking his head nosily through the flap and not being able to get it back. If the telegram had been put by mistake under the front door, Charles told the astonished postmaster, only one thing could have happened. Our cat must have eaten it.

She had. While she watched strategically from the top of the stairs and Aunt Ethel dramatically waited for an explanation at the bottom we found the incriminating evidence – a soggy, well-chewed comer of the envelope – under the hall chair.

What happened then was little short of miraculous. Aunt Ethel was just about to storm out in high dudgeon – she had never liked our animals very much since the day Blondin light-heartedly deposited a small warm trickle down her neck while she was dozing in a chair and this, she informed us icily, was the Last Straw – when Sugieh got up and lumbered slowly down the stairs.

By this time she had a figure like a pear-drop, though up till now it didn't seem to have inconvenienced her very much. Only the previous week she had gone across the garden so fast after a bird she had run into a cloche and cut her nose. Not seriously; just enough to send her even more cross-eyed than usual for a few days looking at the scar. She still, too, climbed trees like the wind without any apparent ill-effect on anybody except Charles who groaned and clutched his head every time she banged her – we hoped – valuable cargo of kittens against a branch.

Now, to our utter astonishment, she crept wearily downstairs as if she could hardly drag herself along, looked Aunt Ethel pathetically in the eye and said 'Waaah!'

Maybe her discomfort was genuine. Maybe it was the result of eating that orange envelope. At any rate we had no more trouble that visit. By night Aunt Ethel slept with Sugieh cradled in her compassionate arms. By day she nursed her on her lap, tenderly stroking her ears and telling her what wicked owners she had, to let the poor little darling be taken advantage of like that.

The poor little darling, wallowing in sympathy as only a Siamese can, acquiesced soulfully in everything she said. To listen to her she had never ever wanted to get married, and we had dragged her down to Dorset by the hair of her innocent little head.

We didn't care. For the first time in months – what was more with Sugieh *and* Aunt Ethel in the house – we had a little peace.

SIX

Enter Four Gladiators

Sugieh had her kittens at the end of March. After a harrowing evening trying to persuade her to have them in a cardboard box lined with newspaper, as recommended by the cat book, while she just as persistently kept getting out of it and marching upstairs flat-eared with indignation at the very idea, they were born just after midnight. On our bed – otherwise, she said, she wouldn't have them at all – while Charles and I sat either side of her, cat book in hand, anxiously awaiting complications.

There were none. Except for the fact that the last one to arrive was half the size of the other three – and that as Charles pointed out to her, was entirely her own fault; he had warned her often enough about rushing up those trees – everything went off quietly, efficiently and speedily.

It was the last time anything was to go off quietly in our house for a long time to come. The next morning we awoke to the depressing discovery that Sugieh, who never did anything by halves, had decided to become the Perfect Mother.

That, while it lasted, was purgatory. For the first few days she hardly left the kittens for a moment. When she wanted food she stood at the top of the stairs and shouted. When we took it up to her she was either back in her basket feeding them as though they were delicate lilies about to fade before her very eyes, or pacing anxiously up and down like a commercial traveller with a train to catch.

The kittens weren't much help either. The only time we did persuade her to come down with us for a while she had hardly had time to cross her eyes at Shorty in the old familiar way before there was a piercing wail from above and she was off up the stairs two at a time shouting look what happened when she left them for a Moment. Now they were being Kidnapped!

Nobody outside a lunatic asylum would have wanted to kidnap that lot, and well she knew it. From the moment they solemnly opened one eye each, days before they should have done, and leered forth at the world like a lot of piratical Fu Manchus it was obvious that they were up to no good. It gave the act a wonderful fillip, though. Much better than the perfect mother, Sugieh was now the perfect mother defending her children from the kidnappers.

Nobody was free from suspicion on this score. When the Rector came to tea she no longer sat on his knee and shed affectionate hairs on his best black trousers. She stayed in the hall giving him sinister looks round the door. When the butcher's boy arrived, instead of running out ahead of everybody else to have a private word about the liver, she glared at him from the window bawling One step Nearer and she'd call the Police.

When the police did come, in the shape of PC McNab bearing a summons for Charles who had not surprisingly driven into town one morning in a coma and left the car under a no-parking sign for two hours, she kicked up such a fuss we weren't at all surprised to see McNab bring out his notebook as soon as he got out into the lane and make an entry that undoubtedly related to breaches of the peace. And when Aunt Ethel came for the weekend specially to see the kittens and we brought them downstairs thinking she at any rate would be all right because she was a friend of Sugieh's, Sugieh nearly went mad.

One after another, as fast as she could, she grabbed the kittens by the scruff of the neck and rushed them dramatically back to the spare room. At bedtime every night for the past year she had complained loudly and bitterly that the spare room was a Vile Prison and she might just as well be Marie Antoinette. Now, it seemed, it was the only place in the world where her kittens were safe. When Aunt Ethel followed apologetically after her with the basket and an odd kitten she had found on the stairs Sugieh, standing bravely on guard in the doorway, growled at her so realistically with her tail bushed and the Siamese fighting ridge raised down her back that Aunt Ethel came downstairs faster than I have ever seen her move in her life and caught the next train home.

Even Sugieh, I think, realized she had overdone it that time. Either that or she was tired of playing at perfect mothers. The next morning, anyway, she dumped the kittens in bed with us at seven o'clock as nonchalantly as if she had never heard of kidnappers, went off into the woods and didn't come back until nine. From then on she made it perfectly clear that they were as much our responsibility as hers.

We have since often wondered whether being dropped on their heads as often as those kittens were in the next few weeks had any connection with the way they grew up. Every morning at least one of them went down with a thump as Sugieh leapt madly on to the bed, stuffing kittens into my arms as fast as she could, and though we wouldn't have gone as far as Sugieh and said that that one was Spoiled – she never bothered to pick up the one she had dropped; just looked at him in annoyance and went off to get another – it was obvious that it couldn't have done them much good. It was significant, too, that the one who got dropped on his head more often than anybody else was Solomon.

Everybody who knows him has at some time or other asked us why on earth we called him Solomon. The answer is that it was his mother's idea of a joke. Knowing full well that we planned to keep a tom out of her first litter as a show cat and to call him – rather brightly, we thought – Solomon Seal, she obligingly produced three toms to give us a choice, watched with intense interest for a couple of weeks as, cat book in hand, we went over their points and debated which we should have – and finally had the biggest laugh of her life when it turned out there was only one we could keep. The one we had written off at the start because he had big feet, ears like a bat and brains to match. All the rest, including the diminutive queen, were Blues.

Solomon, in addition to his other faults, had spotted whiskers. Long before the dusky smudges appeared on his nose and paws to warn us that he was ours for life we had been able to distinguish him from the others by this peculiarity. 'Like an orchid,' said Aunt Ethel, tenderly retrieving him from the coal bucket on her next visit, after she and Sugieh had made it up and Sugieh, dumping her squirming, screeching family into Aunt Ethel's lap by way of a peace-offering, had dropped him overboard as usual. Like bamboo would have been nearer the truth. I have never seen a cat who looked so much like Popski in my life. Bamboo or orchid, it was by his whiskers we recognized him as the one who always fed lying down.

We nearly had a fit the first time we saw it – three kittens feeding away for dear life and standing, to get a better grip, on the fourth, who appeared to be unconscious. After we had dragged him out three times to give him air, however, only to find that within a few minutes he had disappeared once more beneath the scrum we began to get suspicious. When we lifted the top layer of kittens and had a look our suspicions were confirmed. While the others squealed and clawed and battled for position on top, the one with the big feet and spotted whiskers lay blissfully underneath, on his back, with the whole bottom row to himself.

The result of his uninterrupted meals was, of course, that he soon became the biggest kitten of the lot and it was because of this, and the fact that he was Sugieh's favourite, that he was always being dropped.

When she felt like showing off – and it did, though we hated to admit it, make a charming picture – it was always Solomon that she carted down the lane, smirking blandly over his fat white head at the applause. As, however, the outing was essentially in the nature of a film star pushing her offspring round Hyde Park for the benefit of the photographers she usually dropped him on the path as soon as she got back and left him for us to put away. Sometimes she came over the wall and dropped him in the ditch. Invariably she dropped him when she tried some awkward manoeuvre like leaping on to the bed. As he grew bigger she dropped him more and more. When she carried him upstairs his fat white body bumped solidly against every stair. Aunt Ethel, trying fruitlessly to wrest him from Sugieh's grasp on one such occasion, forecast darkly that he would grow up not quite right in the head. She couldn't go wrong there, of course. No Siamese is ever right in the head. Nevertheless it was odd that when Solomon did grow up he had even more peculiarities than an ordinary Siamese – including an overwhelming desire to be dragged round by the scruff of his neck.

It was incredible, seeing that once Sugieh stopped being the perfect mother she acted more as if she needed a course in child care, how those kittens survived. When they wanted washing she washed them so hard they nearly shot out of their skins. When they annoyed her she bit them so hard they screamed for mercy. All except Solomon, who bit her back and then, when she chased him, rolled over and waved his four black socks so disarmingly that he got an extra feed while the others weren't looking.

She had no idea of diet at all. At four weeks old, when according to the book we were supposed to start weaning them on to a patent milk food, she said it wasn't good for them and drank it herself. At six weeks, when we were practically going round the bend because – acting no doubt on her instructions – they shut their eyes and mouths firmly the moment they as much as saw a saucer and we despaired of ever weaning them at all, we found her upstairs one morning surreptitiously feeding them with large lumps of rabbit from her own breakfast and watching proudly while they fought over it like tigers.

She knew quite well that it was wrong. When we lectured her about their delicate stomachs she sat with her ears down, looked at us from under her eyelashes and said it was Solomon. It may well have been, at that. Solomon, who was the one we had worried about most over this feeding business because he was such a big kitten and how he was managing on nothing but his mother's milk we had dared not think, was at that moment standing knee-deep in the middle of the rabbit bowl slurping it back like spaghetti. Solomon, at any rate, was the one chosen – not from malice but because she thought he was so wonderful we couldn't resist him – to bear the blame for everything from then on.

When she stole one of Charles's best yellow socks and showed the delighted kittens how to chew holes up and down the leg till it looked like a colander it was Solomon – when the reaction set in and she realized what she'd done – who was detailed to bring us the remains while the rest sat in trepidation on the landing, ready to run.

When we went to the cinema one night and foolishly left them on our bed because it was cold and they looked so appealing cuddled together on the eiderdown it was Solomon – the rest, led by Sugieh, bolted under the bed the minute they heard us coming up the stairs – who was left in small, solitary splendour to explain the row of holes across the top of a brand new blanket. He had a job doing that. There was only one cat whose mouth would have fitted those round wet holes – and she was flat on her stomach under the bed, pretending she was part of the carpet. There was only one cat, too, strong enough to turn back the bedspread and eiderdown and pull the blanket out. Solomon listened, his big bat ears wide with horror, while we told him who she was, what she was, and what we were going to do to her when we caught her. Something obviously had to be done in a hurry if he was going to save Mum from the tanning of her life – and on the spur of the moment he did it. As I held the blanket up, wailing that it was absolutely useless, he bounced forward, his eyes bright with inspiration, and wiggled a fat black paw through one of the holes. That, he said, was the game they had been playing before we came in. That was the very reason Mum had chewed the holes, and it was terrific fun. Why didn't we have a go?

We were always suckers for that little black pansy face. We did. Within a few seconds the bed was a hilarious mass of kittens charging gleefully up and down the eiderdown and poking paws at us through the blanket while Sugieh, reappearing as if by magic once she knew the danger was past, grabbed Solomon by the scruff of the neck and dropped him lightheartedly off the pillow as a reward.

It wasn't the only reward she gave him. I nearly fainted on the spot when after supper that night he marched proudly into the living room with his spotted whiskers sprouting on one side as exuberantly as a gorse bush – and the other side completely bare. He was only eight weeks old then and we thought they had dropped out as a result of eating too much rabbit. We didn't know Siamese mothers sometimes did that to their favourite kittens when they were particularly pleased with them.

The vet told us – rather shortly, we thought, seeing that he was supposed to like Siamese cats – at half past eleven that night.

SEVEN

Solomon the Great

A few days after that the Smiths brought James to tea for the first time since the kittens were born and Solomon assaulted him. We should have anticipated something like that. Ever since the loss of his whiskers, which he seemed to regard as some sort of accolade, Solomon had been quite unbearable. Head of the Family he said he was, and though the head of the family was more often than not seen disappearing ignominiously round a corner on his back to have his ears washed, it was obviously asking for trouble to have a strange cat in the place.

The snag was, we couldn't ask the Smiths *without* James. They took him everywhere from the post office to the rectory garden party. If they didn't, they said – and as Siamese owners ourselves we quite understood – he kicked up hell, and the neighbours complained.

I bet he wouldn't have complained if he'd known what was coming to him that afternoon. I can see him now, stalking elegantly up the garden path in his bright red harness and stopping every now and then to smell the wallflowers. Sugieh greeting him at the door. A little suspiciously, perhaps – but then Sugieh always greeted people suspiciously; it made social occasions so much more interesting. The pair of them walking side by side into the living room where, said Sugieh, her family was simply *dying* to meet him. And the awful moment when Solomon, his one-sided whiskers simply bristling with hate, shot out from under the table, drew himself up to his full six inches, and spat.

Before it had even started our polite country tea party was bedlam. Sugieh, screaming that he had Attacked her Son, pitched into James. James, who hadn't done a thing but wasn't stopping to argue, took off through the cucumber sandwiches. And Solomon, completely beside himself with excitement, bit Mrs Smith in the leg.

Long after James had been driven home shaking like a leaf and we had swept up the remains of the Copeland bowl that used to stand in the window, Solomon was still telling us about Mrs Smith's leg.

'And after that I bit *James*,' he chanted, sitting on the kitchen table where we were wearily cutting up rabbit for their supper. 'And then I chased him up the *curtains*. And then I bit him *again...*'

Actually he hadn't done anything of the sort. It was Sugieh who bit James. The moment Mrs Smith screamed Solomon had dived under the bureau like a rocket with the rest of the kittens and all we had seen of him for the next twenty minutes was a pair of eyes as round as marbles gazing dumbfounded at the devastation. That, however,

61

was Solomon all over. To add to our other troubles he had turned out to be a feline Walter Mitty.

We usually locked the kittens in the hall when we got their food. Four of them clinging to his legs like Morris bells and Sugieh drooling hungrily in his ear were, as Charles said the day he cut his finger with the chopping knife, more than any man could stand. When the dishes were on the floor, however, and the hall door was opened, it was no ordinary litter of kittens that trooped forth to supper. It was a sheriff's posse with Solomon in the lead. Ears flat, tails raised, they drummed in a solid body through the living room, along the passage and into the kitchen, with Sugieh hard behind charging as enthusiastically – if a little self-consciously – as any of them.

One day the garden door happened to be open as well and Solomon, whose two ambitions in life were to Eat and Be Out, had absent-mindedly galloped the posse out into the yard before he realized it. Father Adams, who was passing at the time, was loud in his admiration of the way in which he skidded to a halt in a cloud of dust, turned, and with a mighty roar led the charge hot-foot back to the feeding bowls. If he'd been a hoss, he said, the little black'un would have made a mighty fine hunter.

Solomon remembered that. The time was to come when he thought he was a horse, and, a pretty fine dance he led us. Meanwhile he was busy being head of the family, and a fine job he made of that too.

In the mornings, when the posse tore out of the front door and up the damson tree so fast it hurt your eyes – half of their time they spent in the damson tree spying down through the leaves at unsuspecting passers-by and the other half they spent with their noses pressed to the hall window complaining there was somebody interesting going by Right This Moment and now they'd Missed Him – it was always Solomon who led the way, shouting This Morning he'd be first at the Top. It was always Solomon, too, who after an initial leap big enough to take him clean over the roof, was left clinging desperately to the trunk about two feet up yelling to us to Catch Him Quick, he was feeling Giddy.

The only time he ever did get to the top – we imagined he must have been carried up bodily by the rush of kittens behind him – he was so overcome with excitement when the Rector went by that he fell out on to his head. Neither of them was hurt, though the Rector – red in the face and the nearest I ever knew him to swearing – said if we *had* to give him a Biblical name it should have been Beelzebub, and after that whenever he came to call he always used to stop at a safe distance and look up into the damson tree before opening the gate. He needn't have worried. Solomon never did it again. Our little black-faced dreamer, though he woke the whole household at five every morning shouting to hurry up and let him out, he knew he could make it This Time, couldn't climb for toffee.

We were always rescuing him from somewhere. If it wasn't from the damson tree it was, more often than not, from the fourth bar of the five-barred gate which led into the lane. Sugieh, who had an eye for effect, was always encouraging her family up there. The idea was obviously to present people walking through the woods with a tableau of Mother and Kittens on a Gate that would absolutely stun them. Very effective it would have been too, if only Solomon had been able to make it. When visitors came past, however, Solomon, wailing with mortification, was always completely and hopelessly stuck on the top bar but one while Sugieh, instead of smirking at them with coy, half-closed eyes from a nest of cuddly kittens as planned, lay flat on her stomach frantically trying to hook him up with her paw.

Failing to climb the damson tree never worried Solomon a scrap, but for some odd psychological reason not being able to get on top of the gate did. In the end he gave up trying. When the other kittens hurled themselves up the gatepost with squeals of delight, to balance-walk across the top with their absurd tails raised like little raft-masts and shrieks of excitement as every now and then somebody slipped and dangled dangerously by one paw, Solomon would stump off all by himself and sit on top of the cotoneaster.

It was a *cotoneaster horizontalis*, it reached quite three feet up the coalhouse wall, and Solomon solemnly sitting on the top of it trying to look as if he had conquered Everest was absolutely heart-rending. Even the other kittens felt sorry for him. One day when Sugieh issued her clarion call to come and be pretty on the gate they all went up the cotoneaster with Solomon instead. Unfortunately Solomon wasn't expecting them and in the heat of the moment he fell off and sprained his paw. Whatever happened, he just couldn't win.

The one thing in which he did surpass the other kittens – other than having the biggest feet and the largest appetite – was his voice. Being Siamese, of course, they all had enormous voices. Even the she-kitten, who was much quieter than her brothers and given to periods of silent contemplation on top of the curtain rail, occasionally startled visitors by emitting a cracked soprano 'Waaaaah' from ceiling level when struck by some particularly profound thought.

Solomon, however, even as a kitten, had a voice only to be compared with a bullfrog. And he never stopped talking. We used to hear him sometimes talking in the middle of the night. When we went in to see what was wrong – we never ignored noises in the night since the time we found Blondin hanging behind a door, trying to suffocate himself in the sleeve-lining of a coat – there, invariably, were the other three kittens snoring away peacefully like little white angels, Sugieh lying on her side with one eye open, obviously wishing him to the devil – and Solomon, bolt upright in the basket, talking to a spider on the wall.

Solomon loved spiders. When he found one too old or infirm to get away he ate it noisily with his mouth open – a habit he had inherited from Sugieh – talking and chewing appreciatively at the same time. It took us quite a time to discover which kitten it was who gave an ecstatic 'Woohoohoo' at intervals while eating rabbit, like a small damp train going through the Rockies, but in the end that turned out to be Solomon too.

He had a vocabulary all his own, which for our own good we quickly learned to understand. A black head appearing round the living room door when we had company and uttering a small but urgent 'Wooooh' meant he was sorry to intrude but the earth-box was dirty, and he wanted it changed in a hurry. Solomon didn't like dirty earth-boxes. A raucous 'Waaow' accompanied by banging noises from the kitchen as he tried valiantly to open the pantry door meant that he was hungry. Loud and prolonged wailing from somewhere up on the hillside behind the cottage meant that Solomon, after setting out with the others all bluff and bustle and Head of the Family, had once more got left behind and wanted to be rescued. The only time he couldn't talk was when he was feeding from Sugieh and if he opened his mouth he lost his place. Then, instead of talking, he waggled his big bat ears so frantically he looked as if he were about to take off.

Solomon, of course, wasn't the only one with character. It was just that as he was the only Seal Point, and we were going to keep him, we naturally noticed him more. His two blue brothers had meanwhile already decided on their careers. They were going to be all-in wrestlers. They were so alike, those two, even we couldn't tell them apart until Solomon bit Sugieh's tail one day and in a fit of pique she decided he wasn't her favourite kitten any more and chewed the whiskers off one of them instead; and they were quite inseparable. Theirs was a peculiar sort of affection, however, as you might expect with a mother like Sugieh. When you came across them they were never sitting lovingly cheek to cheek like the kittens you see on Christmas cards. They were always locked in a close embrace trying hard to kick the daylights out of one another.

Their sister had decided on her career, too. She, when she left us, was going to be a vamp. She was already practising hard on Charles and the boy who did the garden. At night she spent long periods sitting on Charles's knee, gazing into his face with half-closed eyes and swaying with passion when he looked at her. At weekends, while Sidney cut the grass or hoed the potatoes, she languished determinedly round his neck and caused him to slow down his 3/6d.

per hour output by fifty per cent in case she fell off. She held long, intimate conversations with both of them which ceased abruptly when I appeared – and the net result was that when any reference was made to putting the kittens up for sale Charles and Sidney, with their girlfriend preening herself complacently in the background, looked at me as if I was a Gorgon.

There were, however, still a few weeks before we needed to think seriously of selling the kittens. In the meantime, with a sense of relief mixed, on my part, with considerable foreboding, we had arranged to go away for Whitsun. The foreboding arose from the fact that, not liking to ask the Smiths to take them after that catastrophic tea party, we had booked Sugieh and the kittens in at the cattery where she had been mated. It was a place run specially for Siamese, where they would have their own chalet and an enormous run to themselves. Undoubtedly they would be happy there. The only snag was that it was forty miles away.

I worried about that. I worried so much that every morning for a week I woke up at crack of dawn sweating at the very thought. Charles, of course, was as optimistic as ever. Somebody had told him it was possible to get tranquillizers for cats. He would get one, he said, from the vet. He would give it to Sugieh himself. The kittens could travel in a basket on the back seat, and Sugieh would doze quietly on my lap all the way to Halstock. It was as simple as that.

It might have been if he'd asked for a tranquillizer for an elephant. For the first twenty minutes of the journey indeed we did have perfect peace, with Sugieh dreamily gazing over my shoulder at the passing trees and nothing but a gentle scuffling from the back. Then the effect wore off, and in a second we were back in our usual state with those cats. Complete pandemonium. Sugieh was tearing round and round the car like a greyhound screaming not only had she been Kidnapped, she'd been Drugged and where were her precious Children; Charles was shouting to get hold of her for Pete's sake or she'd have us in a crash; the kittens, entering enthusiastically into the fun, had their faces pressed to the airholes of the basket screaming Here they Were, Mum! In here! and I was quietly howling my head off.

How we finished that journey I never knew. We tried going slowly. It made no difference except that it gave passers-by more chance to gawk. We tried going fast – and Sugieh threw herself hysterically under the clutch pedal and nearly killed the lot of us. We put her in the basket with the kittens, thinking they might calm her down, and within fifty yards we had to stop and take her out again before she trampled them to death. Then, no sooner had we got her out and strapped the basket of kittens up again than there was one almighty screech – and Solomon pushed his big, stupid head clean through an airhole and hung there like a stuffed trophy on a wall, choking rapidly and screaming in terror.

That was one of the worst moments of my life. Even Charles seemed to have gone mad. He leapt out of the car, slamming the door so that Sugieh couldn't follow him, and began frantically turning his pockets out on the grass. He was, he shouted, when I asked what he was doing, looking for a penknife. The only way to rescue Solomon was to cut him out. If he did, I shouted back, he'd kill him. You couldn't get a bee's whisker between Solomon's neck and the basket, let alone a penknife. Look!

I put out my hand to show him how firmly Solomon was stuck – and Solomon immediately bit my finger to the bone. If he had enough strength to do that, I thought, he had enough strength to stand what I was going to do now. Without more ado I put my hand flat against his face, shut my eyes and pushed. There was a sort of sucking noise and then, with just enough time to bite another finger for luck, Solomon's head plopped back to safety like a cork from a bottle.

On we went. Dante's Inferno on wheels. The hole in the basket plugged with a scarf, me with my hand wrapped in a towel and Sugieh, the cause of it all, still going round and round the car like a spinning top. At Glastonbury we found a basket shop, bought the biggest hamper they had and shut her in it. Now at least she couldn't race round the car. Instead she expended her energy in screaming louder than ever.

We hardly expected to reach Halstock alive ourselves. We were even more astounded when we reached the kennels and unlocked the baskets. Out, from one, stepped Sugieh, sleek and composed as you like, to greet the Francis's with a gracious bellow. And out, from the other, tumbled four lively kittens fit and fresh as daisies, led by Solomon whom we had expected to find at least a hospital case.

We left them going up and down the wire of their run like caterpillars. We arranged, however, to ring the cattery later that night to see how they were. Charles said they might be suffering from delayed shock. When I heard him talking to Mrs Francis on the 'phone after dinner, and he gave a suppressed groan, I thought he was right. When he put down the receiver, however, he assured me that everything was quite normal. It was just that Sugieh had spotted Rikki and was busily shouting greetings at him the entire length of the cattery while the kittens – as Charles said, grimly, they would let us down – liked their nice, clean, sparkling earth-box so much they had gone to sleep in it.

EIGHT

Downfall of a Church Organ

Cats, said Father Adams, leaning dejectedly on our front gate with his hat tilted over his eyes, was the very devil. From which remark we gathered that, despite all his efforts, Mimi was once more in season.

Three times now she and Ajax had honeymooned uproariously in the attic, and three times Father Adams, praying piously for the patter of tiny paws, had been disappointed. Not only had Mimi failed to outdo the strawberry patch, now the strawberry patch wasn't any good either. A couple of Mimi's earlier suitors had staged a prize fight in it one night to console themselves and trampled all the flowers.

Father Adams said it had him licked. He wouldn't listen to Mrs Adams's theory that it all arose from Ajax already having a wife and steadfastly refusing – as all good husbands should – to look at another cat. He said she was a silly old fool. Not about Ajax having a wife. All Dr Tucker's patients knew Ajax's wife. She was a slender doe-eyed creature called Andromache who had two claims to fame. Firstly that she had bitten the grocer's boy, which was something a good many housewives who had suffered from his cheek would like to have done themselves. And secondly that she was so fond of Ajax that even when she had kittens, which is a time when most queens will attack a tom on sight, she would let him get into the basket with them.

Father Adams knew that was right. He had seen it for himself. Hefty, battle-scarred Ajax tenderly washing the ears of his latest batch of offspring while Andromache sunbathed on the porch. Father Adams's comment on that was that he was an adjectival fool. Catch him putting a flannel to any of his kids' faces while his missus sat round sunning her fat rump.

What Father Adams refused to believe was that Ajax wasn't interested in other females. Cats had more sense, he said. Nobody else believed it either – until a certain strange sequence of events that set everybody wondering. Andromache, coming into season at a time when Ajax was away at the vet's for ear treatment, got out of the pantry window one night and went for a walk with a cat called Nelson who lived at the *Carpenter's Arms*. It was a fine May evening, with the air heady with the scent of hawthorn and a nightingale singing romantically in the copse. Ajax was miles away with penicillin powder in his ear, Nelson was near at hand and ardently amorous – and nine weeks later there were seven black and white kittens with unmistakably Nelsonian squeaks in the basket on the doctor's porch.

Ajax didn't help with that lot. Andromache might rub whiskers with him as much as she liked and say of course they were his, silly, it must have been the penicillin – but he knew black and white when he saw it. He knew Nelson, too. He nearly murdered him one night on the roof of the *Carpenter's Arms* and the next time he went to stay with Mimi there was no nonsense about being faithful to his wife. Six strapping little Ajaxes Mimi had, and Father Adams rubbing his hands with delight; though Mrs Adams rather took the gilt off the gingerbread by continually saying it didn't seem right to her until he asked her what the devil she wanted *him* to do about it. Take the ruddy cats to a Marriage Guidance Council?

It was, of course, complete coincidence. Mimi just happened to be a cat who didn't mate easily. All the same, as people said, it made you think. At the time when Father Adams was leaning on our gate moaning, however, this extraordinary turn of events was still in the future. We, too, were quite oblivious of the tragedy ahead of us. Our problem just then was to fit Sugieh and her tyrannical family into a normal pattern of living.

It took an awful lot of doing. When we had visitors to stay, for instance, we could no longer put them in the spare room. Way back when Sugieh was using it as a nursery we had moved the earth-box up there for convenience – and there, like the Rock of Gibraltar, the kittens expected it to stay. After the embarrassing night when Solomon – who was always much too lazy to use the box before going to bed as Sugieh had taught him, and in consequence invariably had to get up in the early hours – practically tore the door down shouting that he had to get in quick while we in turn tried fruitlessly to persuade him that a box on the landing would do just as well, we gave up putting visitors in there. We slept in it ourselves, kittens, earth-box and all, while the visitors had our room.

We had, too, to be very careful in our choice of guests. It had been one thing to leave Sugieh sitting on the table at mealtimes. We could always nip her off quickly and pretend we didn't know what had come over her – she never did that in the normal way. When, however, a cat and four kittens marched on to the table like a detachment of the Salvation Army as soon as it was laid and grouped themselves solidly round the cruet, it was no good trying to pass that off as an accident. Neither was it any good locking them out in the hall and pretending that was where they usually spent mealtimes. They kicked up such a racket, yelling and banging on the door, that it invariably led to the visitors saying not to shut the little dears out for their sakes and opening the door themselves. Whereupon the little dears would hurl themselves across the room and on to the table with such purpose there could be no doubt even in the dimmest mind as to where they normally sat at mealtimes.

By the time we had weeded out people who objected to kittens peering interestedly into their plates while they ate, people who were squeamish about Solomon sicking up spiders into their laps – that was the worst of spiders, they had such indigestible legs – and people who objected to playing canasta with kittens chewing the cards or poking experimental paws into their ears, there weren't really many we could invite at all.

In some ways it was just as well. The place wasn't looking its best just then anyway. The lamp on the side table, for instance, made from a Georgian candlestick and so lopsided it reminded one of a bad Channel crossing. Romantically-minded visitors might like to imagine its having been dropped down some sweeping Regency staircase in a moment of emotional crisis by a lady who looked like Margaret Lockwood, or used as a weapon in a drunken Regency brawl. The truth was that it got bent one day when four kittens tried to jump it at once in a glorious Grand National round the sitting room, and we were never able to straighten it out.

On the bureau there used to stand a Bristol glass jug, an old toby jug and a china image of a Breton woman spinning. The Bristol jug went west the day after Sugieh brought her family down from the spare room for the first time. When I rushed in after the crash Solomon, sitting on the spot where it had once stood and looking down at the remains with eyes as round as saucers – Sugieh and the others were busily looking out of the window at an ant they swore had just gone round the corner – said it fell off all by itself just as he got there, and why had it gone that funny shape?

We never knew who was responsible for knocking off the head of the Breton spinner. Everybody was at the far end of the vegetable garden busily learning to catch mice when we found her decapitated body lying on the carpet, and when they all trooped back again at lunchtime they assured us they were just as mystified as we were.

After that we took the precaution of putting our one remaining treasure – the toby jug – on the floor when the kittens were around, but we might just as well have left it where it was. Seeing that the top of the bureau was now a nice clear space the gang took to sitting on it *en masse* while they decided what to do next and one day, what with the blue boys having a practice fight while they waited, Solomon saying he ought to sit in front because he was most important and his sister furiously refusing to budge otherwise she couldn't see Charles, the whole lot fell off, landed on the jug like a bomb, and that was the end of that.

Wherever we looked we were surrounded by evidence of our decline and fall. The hide chair in the corner, draped with a tattered car rug. Not to protect it from the kittens – we had long given up hope of that; when they wanted to sharpen their claws they just turned back the rug and got down to it – but to conceal the fact that the stuffing now stuck out in tufts, like some strange African hairdressing style. The patch on the carpet where Solomon sicked up the day he ate two cream cakes at a sitting – and another where Charles dropped the coffee pot the day the she-kitten, who was still hardly bigger than a mouse, lovingly climbed his leg inside his trousers instead of out.

Aunt Ethel was cross about that. Charles ought to have more self-control, she said, and I ought to know better than to give a kitten that age cream cakes.

That was a joke if you like. From the day Solomon found his way on to the table for the first time by the simple expedient of clambering up the curtains and falling off when he got to food level there had never been any need to give him anything. What he fancied he took. The trouble was, what he fancied wasn't always good for him.

Prawns, for instance. Offer Sugieh a prawn and she would close her eyes and say we knew she never ate anything. Offer it to the blue boys and they took one sniff and fought harder than ever. Offer it to the she-kitten, who was so fastidious we wondered she didn't want all her meals sent down from the Dorchester, and she said it was dirty and buried it under a rug. Offer it to Solomon – offer him even a sniff of a prawn's whisker – and, his black face shining with eagerness and his small pink tongue licking nearly up to his eyebrows, he would follow you to the ends of the earth.

Solomon liked garlic sausage, liver sausage, All Bran and string. The first time we saw a piece of string vanish into his mouth, followed by an almighty hiccup which nearly lifted him off the floor, we rang the vet in a panic, but he sighed wearily and said not to worry, particularly if it was Solomon whom he always referred to as the Gannet. Just let nature take its course. It did – then and all the other times we found him eating string, surrounded by an admiring audience of kittens who watched his big act as if he were the star turn at the circus – which, of course, was just what he imagined himself to be. But it never failed to scare us stiff. I was afraid he'd choke and Charles colourfully imagined it winding round his inside like the string on an outboard motor. It took years off us when he made the exciting discovery that he could now get a ping-pong ball right inside his mouth and gave up string-eating to be an Alsatian dog instead.

What with spiders, string, and the occasional butterfly caught napping on a cabbage which he ate wings and all, Solomon was, of course, frequently sick. But never, ever, was he so gloriously sick as the day he ate the cream cakes. It was, in spite of what Aunt Edith said, quite an accident. Hearing the 'phone ring just as I was unpacking the shopping, I had gathered up the fish, chops, sausages and bacon, all of which Solomon had been gloating over saying he liked that, and were we going to have it for tea, and taken them with me for safety. Only the week before I had been idly chatting on the 'phone when a procession, led by the head of the family, passed by on its way to the lawn carrying two pounds of bacon.

I didn't take the bag of cream cakes because Solomon had never shown any interest in them before. Now, as there was nothing else about, he did. Before I had even finished 'phoning he came out to tell me he felt full. As the afternoon wore on he got quieter and quieter and his eyes grew rounder and rounder until eventually he took up his position in the middle of the carpet and we knew there was no doubt about it. Solomon was going to be sick.

Our cats were always sick in the middle of the room. It was a habit started by Sugieh, to make sure she didn't die while we weren't looking, and we were so used to it by this time that we were quite adept at nipping down a newspaper the moment we heard the first burp. All would have been well that time, too, if it hadn't been for the village pest, who chose just that moment to come collecting for the church organ. She came right in, of course. According to Charles that was why she did the collecting. She saw Solomon sitting like a small, sooty-faced elf in the middle of the carpet, and before we could stop her – 'The little Daaaaarling,' she screeched, and swept him tightly to her massive, Scotch-tweeded bosom.

It was too much for Sol. He gave one despairing 'Whoops' and threw up all down her best silk blouse and over the carpet. She was absolutely furious. Even when Solomon said he was sorry but it *was* two whole buns and she *had* squeezed him rather hard round the middle but Never Mind, he felt Much Better now, she wouldn't listen. She marched out without waiting for our contribution and gave the Rector her notice on the spot. People were always insulting her, she said. But when people trained their cats to be sick over her, that was the absolute limit.

That, as Charles used to explain to people for a long time afterwards, was the reason not only for the patch on the sitting-room carpet, but for the fact that the village organ had hardly a black key to its name.

NINE

Call Me Hiawatha

It was just about then that we had a recurrence of the bath trouble. Sugieh's craze for water had vanished after she had her family. She was too busy now, as she was always telling us between frantic toppings and tailings of four protesting kittens, ever to think of herself. So Charles had gone back to leaving the door open while he soaked so that he could hear the wireless, and apart, as he said, from momentary heart failure whenever he heard the posse thunder past like a herd of elephants on its way to the kitchen, bath-time was once more quiet, peaceful and refreshing.

Then, galloping out with the rest of the posse one day, the she-kitten stopped to wash her paw. Solomon had stepped on it, she said, and she didn't want it to be Dirty when she saw Sidney. Taking off after the others like a small blue comet – nobody ever *walked* in our house; just sometimes they whooshed faster than others – she missed the kitchen turning, shot through the bathroom door instead, and before anybody could stop her there was an almighty splash and she was in the water. When I went in Charles was lying back, still clutching the loofah, with an expression of utter resignation on his face, while his girl friend sat dripping happily on his chest telling him how much she loved him.

From then on, even if she was at the far end of the garden talking to Sidney, the moment she heard the bath-tap running she would tear into the house like greased lightning, take up position outside the bathroom door and demand to be let in. A few seconds later Solomon, always ready to join in anything that required using his voice, would roll round the corner and demand to be let in too. Finally the blue boys would arrive to make up the party and the whole lot would sit down and bellow their heads off.

The only way to stop them *was* to let them in, and since we couldn't do that while the water was still in the bath it meant, in order to preserve the peace, bathing in about five seconds flat, pulling the plug as we leapt out, and opening the door to the public the instant the last drop had gurgled down the plug-hole.

They never did anything special in the bath; it was just that they didn't want to miss anything that was going on. Sometimes, said Charles, towelling himself savagely while four smudge-marked faces watched him with interest from the bottom of the bath and Solomon, consumed with curiosity as usual, wanted to know why he took his skin off

81

when he washed, and didn't it hurt when he put it on again. Sometimes he thought he'd get more privacy if he took his bath in Trafalgar Square.

Actually Charles was feeling rather put out with the kittens just then because they had stopped him becoming an archer. Charles had a friend who was keen on archery. One day the pair of them had gone rabbit-shooting with a local farmer and Allister, just for fun, took along his bow and arrows. The farmer took a twenty-yard shot at a rabbit and missed; Allister, taking random aim immediately afterwards, transfixed the rabbit on the spot. 'Lumme! Ruddy Robin 'Ood!' said the farmer, gazing at him in awestruck amazement – and though Allister modestly said it was a complete accident and he couldn't do it again if he tried, Charles had come home with the ambition to be a Robin Hood too.

He started reading books on archery. He bought himself a hat. Though he never wore a hat in the normal way all Charles's sporting activities were highlighted with what he considered to be the appropriate headgear. A balaclava for climbing, for instance, though he was hardly likely to get frostbite in his ears in the Lake District, and all it did was render him stone-deaf when I said I thought we had gone high enough; a scarlet and white striped one made (by me) at top speed one winter when we had snow and Charles, who had been busily reading a book on the frozen North, said pioneers always wore striped caps for woodcutting. Now he had his archer's hat – Sherwood Green, turned up on one side and pinned with a natty sweep of pheasant's feathers that was all his own idea. All he needed now was to learn to shoot – and one evening

Allister came over with his equipment and they went out on the hillside to make a start.

Half an hour later a procession entered the kitchen. Charles first, trembling like a leaf and carrying the blue boys; Sugieh marching alongside with crossed eyes and bushed tail yelling that he'd Nearly Killed Them All and they were going to Leave Home That Very Night; Allister behind, wearing the bewildered expression that marked everybody who ever came up against our Siamese in force; and, far in the rear, Solomon and his sister happily dragging home Charles's hunting hat by its feathers.

What had happened was quite simple. Allister, showing Charles the correct stance and draw, had let fly across the valley and scored a magnificent bull in an oak tree. Charles, using exactly the same stance and draw, had hit a stone two feet ahead of him. The arrow had ricocheted off smartly to the right – and before his horrified eyes had landed slap in the middle of the posse, headed by Solomon, just as it appeared in a body round an outcrop, nosily intent on seeing what Charles was doing. Nobody was hurt. Only, said Charles, he had lost another ten years off his life. Over a mile he and Allister had walked to find a safe place and those cats must have tracked him every inch of the way. If he put the Channel between them, he said bitterly; if he went to *Japan* or somewhere to practise archery, he bet that lot would turn up the moment he took aim and swear he had done it purposely.

Whether they would or not, that was the end of Charles's ambition to be an archer. Allister left the blunted arrow behind – in case, he said, Charles should change his mind, then he could practise with it. But it was the kittens who played with it, not Charles. We kept it under the Welsh dresser, from which it was apt to emerge precipitately at all hours of the day, two kittens dragging it by the feathers like a battering ram and the other two charging behind shrieking it was their turn now and hurry up and get it into the garden.

We took their playing with it for granted, like all their other nefarious pursuits, and anyway we knew the arrow was blunt. But the old lady who used to worry about Sugieh eating scraps in the lane and now felt it incumbent to keep an eye on the way we were bringing up the kittens nearly had a fit the day she looked over the wall and saw them tearing round the garden with it like a pack of Comanche Indians. Did I think it was right, she enquired breathlessly – you could see the dust still settling on the path behind her, she had scuttled up it so fast – to allow those dear little kittens to play with a dangerous missile like that? The wee black one was screaming so hard in the middle of the lawn that indeed she feared he had hurt himself already.

They were a lot safer playing with it than Charles was, I assured her. And if the wee black one let out just one more peep because the others wouldn't let him be Hiawatha and carry the arrow all by himself he was going to get his bottom smacked so hard he wouldn't sit down for days.

If it was any comfort, Charles wouldn't have had much time for archery anyway. He had all he could do that summer trying to keep the garden straight. Now we had not one cat digging holes all over it but five, and as it only needed one to give a speculative scratch for all the others enthusiastically to follow suit, most of the time the garden looked like a map of the moon.

Somewhere or other the kittens, unlike their mother, had discovered that holes could be put to a more practical use than mere play. Visitors going round the garden were continually coming across the embarrassing spectacle of four small kittens squatting solemnly among the roses with four scrappy tails raised like matchsticks and four pairs of round blue eyes fixed on the heavens, earnestly thinking Higher Thoughts.

The trouble was, Solomon could never think Higher Thoughts for long enough. He would start off like the others – tail raised, staring with an air of determined concentration at the sky. Then his gaze would wander and he would spot one of the blue boys similarly engaged a few feet away and, completely forgetting why he was there, start stalking him round a peony. Or he would decide the hole wasn't big enough, start to dig it bigger, and then get sidetracked by a beetle. Beetles always turned up in Solomon's holes and nobody else's. So often, in fact, that we came to the conclusion it must be the same beetle trying to be funny. By the time he had trailed it across the garden – more often than not getting sidetracked again on the way by a bee which Sat on a Flower and Insulted Him or a bird which Flew Over His Head and Said Something Rude – he would completely forget where the first hole was and have to start all over again.

Long after the others had finished Solomon would still be hard at work alternately digging holes and chasing beetles. More times than we could count, the moment we brought the kittens in from the garden he would start raking at the door shouting that he hadn't finished yet and he'd got to go out. And without fail, each time we took pity on him and

85

let him out, no sooner would he have dug another hole and seated himself tearfully on it than that blasted beetle would appear again and we'd be back where we started.

We hadn't done with earth-boxes by any means. Solomon usually finished up on one in the end, having been dragged screeching from the garden half an hour after everybody else. Sugieh always used one. It wasn't ladylike to use the garden, she said, and where the kittens had picked up such a dreadful habit she didn't know. Everybody used it before going to bed. Everybody that is, except Solomon, who could usually be heard trying to dig through the bottom of his box at two o'clock in the morning.

This consituted another problem in the complicated business of cat-keeping. Getting the earth for the earth-boxes. Perhaps hazard is a better word than problem. The problem was, after all, solved simply enough by me, twice a week, after a heated argument with Charles as to why he couldn't go, trundling off to the woods with wheelbarrow and spade and getting a load of leaf-mould. The hazard was that all the cats insisted on coming too.

Try as I might I could never get away unnoticed. Sometimes I left the wheelbarrow outside in the lane waiting for an opportune moment to sneak out and run for it. It was no use. Always somebody was watching. Hidden in the lilac that drooped so conveniently over a corner of the coalhouse roof; lurking ostentatiously round the corner of the woodshed; or, if it was Solomon, simply sitting in the wheelbarrow waiting to go.

It was bad enough on the outward journey. Kittens in the wheelbarrow; kittens tumbling out of the wheelbarrow; Sugieh marching alongside shouting to everybody she passed to Look At Us Going for the Leaf-Mould; and after the first few minutes somebody, usually Solomon, wailing frantically far in the rear to Wait For Him, He'd Got Left Behind!

On the outward journey, however, they did at least know they were going *somewhere*, and in case it should be somewhere interesting – none of that lot were going to miss anything if they could help it – we usually got there more or less as a unit. The real trouble started on the way back, when they realized with dismay that they were only going home.

Then they started shinning up every tree they came to, saying they were going to stay there and be little birds – all except Solomon, who sat at the bottom and said he was going to be a mushroom. They hid in the long grass and then, while I called them frantically in one part of the meadow, suddenly came leaping over the moon-daisies like a troop of kangaroos, from a different direction altogether. They prepared endless traps for one another. What with the stealthy stalking of the ambusher and the even stealthier approach of the victim that game could be guaranteed to take ages, particularly if the victim was the she-kitten who didn't like being jumped on and immediately started going back the other way. Even when we got back to civilization they wouldn't behave. Then they dawdled at everybody's front gate, either bawling for me to go back for them, Sugieh included, because they were Afraid to Go Past – or, if there was something interesting inside, like a baby in a pram or an open front door, marching in in a body and having a look.

Often when I got back from one of those trips I was so exhausted I had to go and lie down to reassemble my shattered nerves. Not that I got much rest. If I left the cats in the garden I lay there wondering what they were up to. Once, indeed, I came down to investigate an unnatural silence just in time to spot them marching away into the distance, off to do the leaf-mould walk all over again. If I took them upstairs with me they either played tag all over the bed or sat heavily on me in a body and said they were going to sleep as well. If I left them downstairs, that was usually the signal for Sugieh to show them how to knock down Shorty.

I always got up and reeled wearily down the stairs when I heard the crash, just in case – and it was fortunate that I did. One day I went down to find that the armchair was not in its usual position and Shorty, tail-less as usual and completely grounded, was running madly round on the floor trying to face up to a circle of all four kittens at once while Sugieh, seated maternally on the chair-arm, encouraged them with soft cries to play with the pretty birdie, he couldn't run away.

I remember that so well because it was the last adventure they had as a family. The next day one of the blue boys, after a final game that brought a stupid lump to my throat as I saw his small paw poking excitedly at his brothers and sister through the air-holes of his basket, went to his new home. And the day after that Sugieh – suddenly, tragically, unbelievably – was dead.

TEN

The Giant-Killer

Sugieh died after an operation for spaying. We had decided not to breed any more kittens. It wasn't that we had grown tired of them. Even though they had wrecked the house and shattered our nerves, there was nothing we would have liked more than to go on raising noisy, despotic, fascinating Siamese for ever.

From the practical point of view, however, we found that in our remote part of the country it wasn't easy to sell the kittens; and that the people who did make enquiries nearly dropped dead when we asked four guineas each. They expected kittens, like cabbage plants, to be cheaper in the country. One woman said outright that the Siamese cat business was a racket. People with ordinary kittens, she said, were only too glad to give them away. Cats bred like flies, kittens cost nothing to rear, and where was the difference she would like to know?

The difference was that we paid a lot more than four guineas for Sugieh. We had also paid to have her mated to a first-class tom and the kittens had been raised, not on scraps or bread and milk, but on the properly-balanced diet that is essential for Siamese. Ordinary kittens leave their mothers at four to six weeks, but Siamese kittens are slow developers and no breeder worthy of the name would sell a Siamese kitten under ten to twelve weeks old.

The first of the blue boys was fourteen weeks old when he left us, and though it hadn't been as much in the early days, of course, by that time the four kittens and Sugieh were costing us more than thirty shillings a week to feed. Including the cost of having them inoculated against feline gastro-enteritis – and that, too, was essential; the mortality among Siamese kittens from that disease was terribly high – if we sold them at four guineas we would barely break even.

Obviously we couldn't go on breeding them to sell at a loss. We were told that breeders often had this trouble with their first litter, and that once we became known we would sell them quite easily. Against that, however, we weighed the fact that we had bought Sugieh primarily as a pet, and that since having the kittens she had been so preoccupied with them she had undoubtedly grown away from us. She had become very thin and nervous too. We didn't want her to be like that all her life. We decided that we would prefer to keep her and Solomon as pets. So we had her spayed – an operation which, in these days, is perfectly safe ninety-nine times out of a hundred. Mimi, when she had the same operation later on, came through it perfectly. But Sugieh died.

Numbly we buried her under the apple tree where only the night before, her blue fur ruffling in the breeze, we had watched her playing tag with her three remaining kittens. We shut them in while we buried her so that they shouldn't see her go; but when we went back into the house and what was left of the posse came galloping out to greet us we felt as if we were murderers.

We never forgot Sugieh. For a while, indeed, we thought of buying back the other blue boy and keeping her family together; but that was impossible. Not only would the cost of feeding them, when they grew up, have been colossal but – putting sentimentality aside – *four* of them, taking up all the eiderdown, bossing us round the place and getting us into trouble at every turn… No. It would have been too much.

So the second blue boy went to friends over whom, like a true Siamese despot, he lorded it from the start. They christened him Ming, which was a complete misnomer by any standards. He neither looked the least bit fragile himself, nor had any regard for anything that was. Every time we heard of him after that he had just smashed something fresh. He told them, they said, that his family did that every day when he was home. The she-kitten stayed on with us to take the place of her mother and was – more aptly than we realized at the time – christened Sheba. And Solomon adopted me as his Mum.

Sheba hardly missed her mother at all. Sugieh had much preferred her sons anyway, and Sheba had long since transferred her affections to Charles, whom she could enslave with one blink of her blue eyelashes any time she liked. But Solomon had been his mother's favourite, and he missed her dreadfully. The night she died we let the kittens come to bed with us, as much for our consolation as for theirs. Sheba and the blue boy settled themselves methodically on a corner of the eiderdown, washed each other's ears and fell asleep at once. Solomon, however, spent a long time plodding forlornly up and down the bed saying he was hungry – at fourteen weeks he, alone of all the kittens, had still not been completely weaned – until at last he gave up the search, crept into my arms, and, with a small, sad 'Wooh', said if Sugieh didn't want him any more, then *I* had better be his Mum.

Touching though it was, being Solomon's Mum had its snags. It meant, among other things, having to sleep cheek to cheek with him any time he and his sister managed – by hiding under the bed or looking particularly forlorn – to avoid being shut in the spare room for the night. Sheba, after one brief attempt at cuddling up to Charles, took to sleeping on top of the wardrobe. Nobody fidgeted up there, she said.

Not so Solomon. Whichever way I turned, if I opened an eye in the middle of the night there would be a small black head on my pillow, bat ears semaphoring gently as he slept, snuggled as close as he could get to mine. Solomon had loved his Mum, and so had I, and it seemed the least I could do to comfort him. I drew the line at some things though. The nights he had fish or garlic sausage for supper, Solomon – wail woefully though he might about being an Orphan and people ought to be Kind to him – slept next door.

Being Solomon's Mum also meant that I was the only one he would come to when called (though that was counter-balanced by Charles being the only one who had any influence over Sheba); and that I was expected to rescue him from any trouble he got into. With Solomon still the indefatigable Walter Mitty of the family, that was pretty well a full-time job.

The first thing he did, free from Sugieh's stern, if spasmodic control, was to start a campaign against dogs. From now on, he said, no dog would be allowed even to look through the gate. If they did, by gosh, they saw something that struck terror into their hearts. Solomon looking back at them.

Actually, while Sheba could look very fierce indeed when she was annoyed – she had a way of flattening her ears so far down towards her eyebrows it looked as if she were wearing a cloth cap, and when she crossed her eyes as well the effect was really horrible – all Solomon succeeded in doing was looking worried. It worked though. The Rector's wife and her Pekinese – he extended his activities in their case to crawling under the gate and following them up the lane, walking sideways like a crab with his back arched and threatening to attack – were absolutely terrified of him. He scored a monumental victory over a Dalmatian called Simon who, so his owner told me, had been badly scratched as a pup and had been scared stiff of cats ever since. Simon, sniffing soulfully at a spray of cow parsley just outside the gate, nearly fainted on the spot when he saw Solomon squinting myopically at him round his own back leg. He gave one anguished yelp and fled up the hill as if the devil were after him, after which we heard so much from Solomon about

All the Dogs being Afraid of Him, Even the Ones as big as Elephants, that Sheba got fed up and went and sat on the sitting room door to teach him a lesson.

That was another thing we had to remember now. Always to look at the tops of doors before shutting them, in case Sheba was sitting up there to annoy Solomon. Whenever she got browned off with his swanking, or with his knocking her down to show he was bigger than she was, she just leapt lightly on to the top of the nearest door and looked at him with meaning.

Solomon knew what the meaning was, all right. She was reminding him that he couldn't jump, and it never failed to cut him to the quick. Forgetting all about being most important and dogs as big as elephants, he would sit on the back of an armchair, which was the nearest he could get to her, and wail with mortification. Except, that is, for the day he had his bright idea. Half-way through the first howl he got down off the chair, tore upstairs, and after a series of muffled thumps that sounded as if the roof were coming in, announced with a bellow that he was on a door too. Come and see! He was indeed. The thumps had been him heaving himself laboriously up Charles's dressing gown which hung behind the bedroom door, and now he was balanced shakily but triumphantly on the top. Charles and I praised him extravagantly and pretended not to notice the dressing gown, but there was nothing magnanimous about Sheba. She went round behind the door, sniffed pointedly at the hem, and – as she rode away down the stairs again on Charles's shoulder, leaving Solomon to his triumph, opened her little blue mouth and said something that could only be interpreted as 'Yah!'

She was right, too. No sooner had we reached the bottom than there was another almighty yell from upstairs. Only this time it wasn't triumph. Solomon, marooned at a dizzy height of six feet and unable to work out how to utilize the dressing gown for the descent, was issuing the old familiar call for somebody to rescue him quick, he couldn't get down.

Shortly after that Solomon gave up his campaign against dogs. One of them chased him up a tree and Solomon, for the first and only time in his life, went right to the very top. Six feet up would have done, but Solly wasn't taking any chances. Right to the top Mum had always said, and right to the top he went. Unfortunately he chose a forty-foot fir tree on a sloping hillside, and we had to call out the fire brigade to get him down again. 'Looks like a liddle star on a Christmas tree, don' 'ee,' said the man who worked the winch, gazing tenderly up through the branches to where old Bat-Ears, clinging panic-stricken to the tip, swayed sadly to and fro against the evening sky. That wasn't what the man who had to go up the ladder said. He said if he was us he'd keep him in a cage. It taught Solomon a lesson, though. He never hunted dogs again. He took up chasing cats instead, and Sheba came down out of the damson tree and joined him.

Their chief quarry was a tortoiseshell called Annie, who lived with an old lady further down the lane. Sugieh, as a kitten, had had a sort of Topsy and Eva friendship with Annie, and although they didn't have much to do with one another after they grew up and Sugieh realized she was a Siamese, Annie often used to sit on our garden wall watching the kittens play. Not, however, after Solomon had issued his edict about no cats being allowed to look in either. Any time we saw Annie after that she was playing the lead in a sort of Willow Pattern procession that went past our front gate about a dozen times a day. Annie first, flat on her stomach and looking hauntedly over her shoulder; Solomon, on his stomach too, with his spotted whiskers bushed out like a walrus, slinking stealthily along behind like a musical comedy spy; and Sheba, carefully avoiding the puddles and looking to see if Charles was watching, bringing up the rear.

They had no mercy on anybody. Well, hardly anybody. When Mimi turned round one day in the lane, saw them slinking along behind her and gave them a cuff each alongside the ear they decided to make an exception in her case, seeing that she was a Siamese too. But there was nothing soft about them the day they found a stray tabby queen and her kitten sheltering, after a heavy night's rain, under a row of cloches in the garden. When I, touched by the sight of the tiny, homeless kitten asleep on the bare earth, took out some bread and milk and put it under the cloche they stared at me incredulously. Didn't I know, they said, that these were Dangerous Characters? In Our Garden? Probably going to Eat All Our Food? Probably got Fleas too, added Sheba, who was getting more like her mother every day. The moment the mother cat, unnerved by their awful threats, slunk out at the far end of the cloches and over the wall, Solomon and Sheba went into action. In through the near end they marched, growled fiercely at the kitten – Sheba with her cloth cap look and crossed eyes for good measure – and ate his bread and milk. That showed him, by Jove. He took off as fast as his small white paws would carry him, screaming frantically for his Mum. We never saw *him* again.

Nemesis caught up with them in the end, of course. At least it caught up with Solomon. Sheba was up a tree at the time. She kept telling him the black and white tom from the farm was one of those nasty cats Mum had warned them about, but he wouldn't listen. Jack the Giant-Killer he said he was, and as fast as I brought him back to the safety of the garden, back, to sit in the lane and spit, he went.

When the tom, after staring at Solomon incredulously for nearly an hour, said he didn't believe it and strolled off into the woods Solomon was beside himself with triumph. Long after he had followed his quarry up into the undergrowth we could hear him telling the world how valiant he was, and how All the Cats, Even the Ones as big as Elephants, were afraid of him.

A few minutes later there was a hideous scream and the pair of them bounded out of the woods like shots from a gun. To our amazement – for from the noise we thought he'd murdered Sol: Sheba, indeed, was as high as she could get in the damson tree saying now she was our only comfort she'd better take special care of herself – the tom was in the lead. We caught just one glimpse of him as he hit the road before streaking off up the hill in a cloud of dust, and he looked as if he had seen a ghost. The funny thing was, Solomon was in exactly the same state. Though he didn't appear to be damaged in any way he fled indoors and hid under the bed.

Later that night, a sad little Solomon indeed, he crept out to take a saucer of milk and we discovered what had happened. It couldn't have happened to anybody but him. Trying to spit, talk and look fearsome at the same time he had bitten clean through his own tongue. It didn't inconvenience him in any way, though it healed as forked as a lizard's. It would have taken a lot more than that to stop Solomon eating or talking. But it stopped him chasing the tom. Any time the enemy appeared in sight after that – proceeding very warily because he thought Solomon had beaten *him* and he didn't want another meeting – we knew exactly where to find the giant-killer. In our bedroom, hiding under the eiderdown.

ELEVEN

Beshrewed

Sometimes we wondered what we had done to deserve those cats. Take, for instance, the American we met in Florence. It was all very well for her to stand in front of Lippi's portrait with her hands clasped in ecstasy, declaiming Browning's poem about him at the top of her voice. It was all very well for her to feel so deeply about Savonarola she nearly passed out at the first sight of St Mark's. She had time for such things. She wasn't so addled by a pair of slant-eyed tyrants that she'd booked her train reservations for the wrong day. She wasn't still suffering from the effects of the latest trip to the cattery with Sheba bawling to Charles to Spare Her every inch of the way and Solomon eating car rugs as hard as he could go. Her cats knew how to behave themselves.

She had three of them, all Siamese. In winter they lived graciously in a New York apartment and never dreamed of trying to tear the doors down to get out. In the summer, together with a Boxer, a 'cello, a sewing machine and her husband, who was a member of the New York Philharmonic Orchestra, they drove in an estate wagon up to Maine where they spent three happy months hunting in the New England woods.

They were simply wunnerful on the trip, she said. The only snag was that as it was a five hundred mile journey they had to stay at a motel overnight, and while dogs were allowed in motels they never knew how the proprietor might react to cats. They had overcome that, she said, by having three wicker travelling baskets made to look – we admired the touch – like Gladstone bags. When they arrived at the motel the cats were popped into the bags, cautioned to be quiet, and carried in with the luggage.

'And are they quiet?' I asked, with a horrible vision of Solomon being carried screaming into the cattery in his basket, long black paws flailing out of every hole he could find so that it looked as if we had captured an angry octopus.

'Oh sure,' she said. 'After they've cased the joint to make sure it's all right they settle down so quiet you'd never know they were there. They wanna go to Maine as much as we do.'

While we still had our mouths open she told us about Clancy. That, as she said herself, was really something. Clancy was a champion Siamese tom belonging to a friend of hers back home. He was handsome, he was affectionate, and he fathered such wonderful kittens that his services were in demand all over New York. The trouble was he had to eat so much raw beef to keep his strength up that his food bill was colossal, and nothing like balanced by his stud fees. It was a problem in economics that had Clancy's owner's husband, who was a stockbroker – of Scottish descent, said our friend, anxious that we shouldn't get the wrong angle – quite worried for a while. Then he found a solution. He opened a stockbroking account in Clancy's own name, all his stud fees were invested in it, and Clancy was now the richest cat on the New York Exchange. Didn't we think, she asked, finishing her coffee at a gulp – she had a busy afternoon ahead of her, buying tablecloths and seeing the place where Savonarola was burned – that that was wunnerful? We said it sure was.

Our cats might not be wizards of the Stock Market but there was little doubt that they would have made wonderful actors. Sheba could melt the stoniest heart with her fragile, wide-eyed innocence, deceptive though it was; and Solomon, when he was sitting down and you couldn't see his spindly legs, which were now so long he walked like a camel, could look unbelievably tragic.

As a combination they were irresistible, and well they knew it. Nobody would think, when we had visitors and they sat side by side on the hearth-rug with Sheba demurely reaching up to wash Solomon's ears and Solomon occasionally retaliating with an affectionate slurp that nearly knocked her off her feet, that right before the doorbell rang they had been fighting like a couple of alley cats over who was going to have first place on Charles's lap. Nobody would think – seeing them trotting meekly down the hill behind the Rector, who had for the umpteenth time that week found them sitting outside his front gate wailing that they were lost – that to their dear little minds it was the side-splitting equivalent of ringing doorbells and running away. Nobody except us, who had seen them marching determinedly up the hill in the first place, ignoring our appeals to come back and changing their pace to a forlorn meander before our very eyes as they rounded the corner.

And even we were flabbergasted when we heard that when we were at the office they could be seen in the hall window every afternoon at four-thirty, gazing wistfully up the hill and imploring passers-by to tell them when we were coming home. When we got in just after five they were always Sound Asleep in an armchair and there was such an exhibition of opening one eye, yawning and complete astonishment that we were back so soon that we could hardly believe it. Until we went home one night to find them Sound Asleep and the hall curtains lying in their water bowl. Nobody misses anything in the country and the woman who told us how that happened – it was just after four and Solomon, presumably limbering up for the show at four-thirty, was swinging upside down on one of the curtains like a monkey – said she hoped he hadn't hurt himself but he went down with an awful bang.

Solomon was all right. It was just that his weight – his favourite pastime just then was eating and he was, I regret to say, familiarly known as Podgebelly – had brought down not only the curtains but the blocks on which they were screwed to the wall as well. He was in any case not entirely to blame. He was only copying Sheba, who often swung upside down on the curtains to amuse Charles.

He was always copying Sheba. Brash though he was, always noisy, always in trouble – underneath it all Solomon was a small, wistful clown, valiantly striving to be most important and best at everything and pathetically conscious that he was not. Sheba, on the other hand, was a veritable prodigy. Frail and tiny as a flower, she could run like the wind, climb like a monkey, and had the stamina of an ox.

What Solomon envied most was her prowess as a hunter. Solomon was hopeless at hunting. Not because of any physical incapacity but because he just hadn't got a clue in his big, bat-brained head. His idea of catching mice in the garden wall was not, like Sheba, to lie patiently in wait for them. That, he said, was girl's stuff. He blew threateningly down the hole and then, when they wouldn't come out and fight like men, thrust in a long black paw and tried to hook 'em out.

Any time he did sit down with her to watch something – very impressive he looked too; head narrowed, dark nose pointing eagerly, every inch Rin-Tin-Tin on the trail – five minutes without action and Solomon was either sound asleep from sheer boredom or, with his head swivelled back to front, busy talking to a passing butterfly.

The result was that while his sister slaughtered mice and shrews by the dozen, Solomon never caught anything first-hand in his life. Unless you count his snake, which was quite six inches long, and he got so excited when he found it that he jumped on its tail instead of its head and it got away.

It was, we knew, his secret sorrow. The look on his face as he watched Sheba prancing and posturing with her trophies before laying them Eastern-fashion at our feet was pathetic. Sometimes, when he could bear it no longer, he would dawdle up on his long, sad, spidery legs, head down so that Sheba shouldn't see what he was carrying, and present us with a soggy leaf. Then he would sit down and look soulfully up into our faces, imploring us with all his small Siamese heart to make believe that he had caught something too. It was a heart-rending scene – marred only by the fact that the moment he managed to grab Sheba's booty away from her, Solomon was a different cat altogether.

Then, tossing it high into the air, leaping after it and catching it in his paws, flinging it spectacularly across the room – it was just as well to be out of range when he got to that stage; Charles once fielded a boundary right in his cup and it put him off tea for days – Solomon's ego was back with a bang.

It was His Mouse, he said, panting fiercely over the corpse at Sheba and daring her to pant back. But you couldn't catch Sheba out. She just sat smirking at Charles saying didn't Solomon look silly showing off like that and it was only an old one anyway. It was His Mouse, he said, crouching defensively over it when the Rector called – adding, quite untroubled by conscience, that he'd Caught It All Himself. He went on yelling about it being his mouse until either everybody was fed to the teeth and Sheba went and sat on a door or else, taking him completely by surprise – on one occasion indeed frightening him so much he leapt several feet into the air – the mouse got up and ran away.

Once it happened with a field mouse which, while Solomon was telling the milkman how he caught it, nipped smartly round the corner and under a cupboard door. We never did find out what happened to that one, except that the next time Charles took his duffel coat out of the cupboard all the toggles fell off.

It happened several times with shrews. What with live ones looking for the way out and dead ones tucked tidily under the hall rug by Sheba – she was pressing them, she said, for her collection, and it didn't matter if we stepped on them one bit – in the end we got to know quite a lot about shrews.

Before we had the cats I had only seen one live shrew in my life, and that was the one which came tearing round the corner where I had just dug away a flower border from the side of the cottage, only to discover that he no longer had a home to go to. I can see him now scuttling to and fro on the cobbles, searching incredulously for his front door, and me scuttling conscience-stricken behind him, wondering whether it was safe to pick him up and help him find a new one. Some people said shrews were so nervous they died if you touched them. Others said they bit. I never learned who was right from that one. In the end my nerve failed me and I went indoors while he made up his own mind what to do. I learned soon enough when we had Solomon and Sheba, though. Shrews bite.

Both Charles and I were bitten at different times. I by one which Solomon had delightedly cornered in the kitchen after its first escape – he was talking to it and when I put out a nervous hand to pick it up that must have been the last straw; squealing with rage it leapt fiercely at me and bit me in the finger. And Charles by one which, as it looked a little battered, we had put in a box lined with leaves and grass and locked in the bathroom to see if it would revive. It did. When Charles went in to look at it a while later it was trying, mad with temper, to climb out of the box, and when he put out a helping hand he got bitten too. He yelled so hard that

Sheba, who was looking under the bathroom door at the time, fled out of the house in terror and up the damson tree, Solomon hid under the bed and I dropped the pastry bowl. Not that a shrew's bite is very big, of course. Hardly more than a pin-prick. It was just, said Charles, appearing with a large strip of sticking plaster round his finger and the shrew, ready for release, bouncing furiously up and down in the toe of a sock, that it was so unexpected.

Even more unexpected was the shrew that actually lived with us for four days. This was a good deal later, when Sheba, finding that if she came in with anything alive we took it away from her, had developed the habit of sneaking her trophies up on to our bed. There she could do her nature study against a background of nice clean eiderdown, with the advantage that when she heard us coming she had only to pick up her victim and dive under the bed and we couldn't touch her. This particular shrew, however, she took up to the bed while there was still somebody in it. Aunt Louisa. (Although we had only the two cats now we still put guests in our room and slept in the spare room ourselves. It saved a lot of argument with Solomon.) And Aunt Louisa, when she saw the shrew, let out such a scream that Sheba, who was normally as. imperturbable as an iceberg, dropped it in amazement and it got away.

I know all about shrews eating several times their own weight of food a day and it being impossible to keep them in captivity. Sidney, who has a natural countryman's interest in such things, told me he had seen it on the Telly. Impossible or not, that shrew appeared so often during the next four days even Sheba began to look shaken when she saw it. Upstairs – cruising like a small grey submarine across the landing or through the bedrooms. Downstairs – ambling airily out from under the chest or the cupboard door and across the carpet. We never caught it, though it never hurried. Charles refused to touch any of Sheba's shrews now, without gloves, and by the time he had fetched them – I refused to touch it at all – it had always vanished, while the cats were so embarrassed they had obviously decided the best thing to do was to ignore it.

Several times when I went to change Solomon's earth-box I found it lurking under the rim. Charles said that was probably how it kept alive, eating worms and insects out of the earth-box. That seemed unlikely. If there were any worms or insects around Solomon would have eaten them himself. It put a new responsibility on me, though. Not wishing to have its death on my conscience, every time I changed the box I felt obliged to put down a handful of grass as well.

Aunt Louisa said I took after Grandma and both of us were crazy. Solomon enquired indignantly how he could ignore what was under his earth-box if I fed it right under his nose and said that until it went he was going to use the garden. Charles took to surreptitiously shaking his shoes in the morning before he put them on. We felt like running up the Union Jack when, on the evening of the fourth day, the shrew ambled down the porch step and out of our lives for ever.

TWELVE

Death of a Fur Coat

The day Sheba chased a gnat behind the picture over the bureau and left a row of black footprints up the wall Charles said it wasn't fair to blame the cats for everything. It wasn't her fault, he said, that when it flew past she happened to be looking up the chimney and had her paws covered in soot. I must remember that Siamese were not as other cats, and make allowance for their verve and curiosity.

He didn't say that when we put down the new stair carpet and Solomon, busily showing Sheba how Strong he was, ripped the daylights out of the bottom tread while we were still hammering down the top. He said Solomon was a damblasted little pest and if he wasn't careful he'd end up in the Cats' Home. Neither did it improve matters when I, to protect the rest of the carpet until Solomon got tired of sharpening his claws on it, made a set of stair pads out of folded copies of *The Times*. The idea was to put a pad on each stair whenever we were going out. It worked for a few days – then one morning Charles, dashing up at the last moment to fetch his wallet, slipped on the top copy and slid from top to bottom on his neck. Both Solomon and I were in the dog-house then, and although it didn't worry me unduly – Charles, who is six feet tall, falls down the cottage stairs, which are steep and narrow, quite regularly, and I would get the blame even if I were on the top of Everest at the time – Solomon was quite put out about it.

While Sheba comforted Charles in the hall, walking up and down on his stomach and asking anxiously if he were Dead, Solomon sat at the top of the stairs delivering a long Siamese monologue about the injustice of it all. Sheba Clawed Things, he said, and Nobody Complained About Her. She did too. The underside of the spare room armchair sagged like a jelly bag where Sheba, when she first woke up in the morning, dragged herself round and round on her back by way of exercise – and all Charles said about that was that we had to make allowances for her high spirits.

She Knocked Things Down and Hit People Too, wailed Solomon. You could tell when he got to that bit by the pitch of his voice. Always powerful, it rose to an ear-shattering roar when he was in the right and knew it. Solomon didn't knock things down and hit people. He couldn't climb high enough to start with. But Sheba, shinning like a mountain goat up the bookshelves either side of the fireplace, was always bombarding unwary visitors with dislodged encyclopaedias or law books. Lately I had begun to wonder whether that, too, was quite the accident she claimed it to be. It had certainly been no accident the night I was just in time to stop her crowning Solomon with a Benares brass pitcher. When I caught her she was standing on the arm of a chair trying as hard as she could to hook it off the mantelpiece with her paw while he, stretched out full length to warm his stomach, lay innocently asleep on the rug below.

Now, craning his neck over the landing to make sure everybody heard him, Solomon continued his tale of woe. Charles was Clumsy, he wailed, staring reproachfully down at the spot where Sheba, relieved to find that Charles was good for a few more years yet, was making the most of the occasion by treading vigorously on his waistcoat and assuring him that she was a good girl. Charles would have Fallen Down the Stairs even without the newspapers, yelled Solomon. Charles Fell Over Everything. Charles Fell Off the Ladder only last Saturday. Nobody, said Solomon, with the mournful wail-cum-sniffle which meant that at that moment he was feeling particularly hard done by, could blame him for that. Charles had done it All By Himself.

Charles had indeed. He had been painting the eaves of the cottage, perched on the sloping hall roof, on a ladder that had a cracked leg and was – despite Father Adams's warning that he knew several blokes who had killed themselves like that – suspended by faith and a piece of ancient rope from the chimney stack. Charles's own version of what happened was that he was just reaching up to put on the last brushful of paint, thinking to himself (he was given to making up tense little dramas to amuse himself while he worked) 'And at that moment, just as he reached out for the final handhold, there was a sharp crack of breaking rope and he fell like a stone into the abyss below' – when the rope did break. Not with a sharp crack. It unravelled slowly and sadistically before his very eyes as he stood helplessly on the top rung. He didn't fall into any abyss either. He landed on the hall roof with a thump that shook the cottage to its poor old foundations. When I rushed out, convinced that I was a widow at last, he was sitting despondently on the roof in a pool of pale blue paint while, standing side by side on top of the coalhouse, craning their necks like a couple of spectators at a Lord Mayor's Show, Solomon and Sheba anxiously enquired what he wanted to do that for.

Charles said I might not believe it, but as he slid down the roof after the crash he had seen – actually *seen* – that pair gallop down the path and scramble up on to the coalhouse as if it were a grandstand. I believed it all right. So often in trouble themselves, there was nothing they liked better than sitting smugly by, tails wrapped primly round their front paws and expressions of pained incredulity on their faces, when somebody else was in the soup. I remember once when a dog chased a neighbour's kitten up the electricity post outside our garden wall. Solomon was hardly in a position to talk, after the incident of the fire brigade, while Sheba had lately developed her mother's habit of demanding to be rescued by Charles from every tree she came across. It made no difference. While Charles and I tried to solve the problem of getting a ladder safely balanced against the rounded post they sat side by side at the foot, their necks stuck out like giraffes to emphasize What A Long Way Up She Was, their eyes round as bottle stops, yelling encouragingly up at her that she was Very

Silly To Do A Thing Like That and They Didn't Suppose We'd Ever Get Her Down Again. The fact that no sooner had Charles rescued the kitten than he had to go up again to fetch Solomon, who had meanwhile climbed the ladder himself by way of an experiment and was now stuck half-way up bellowing his own head off, was quite incidental. It still left Sheba at the bottom nattering away happily about what a long way up *he* was and she didn't suppose we'd ever get *him* down either.

It was inevitable, of course, that their rubber-necking would one day lead them into trouble. It happened at a time when we had new neighbours in the next cottage and Sol and Sheba, consumed with their usual curiosity, were going up every day to see how they were getting on. We warned the people not to encourage them. Disaster, we said, would unfailingly follow. Solomon would wreck their stair carpet or raid their pantry and Sheba would either go up their chimney or fall down their lavatory. They wouldn't listen. They hadn't met any Siamese before and they were fascinated, they said, by the way our two marched one behind the other down the garden path, greeted them with an airy bellow and proceeded to inspect the place as if they owned it. Which, so far as we could see, made it entirely the Westons' own fault when they tried to fill their water-butt during a drought by means of a hose-pipe sneaking illicitly through the delphiniums and lupins to the kitchen tap and Solomon and Sheba promptly gave them away to the entire village by sitting on the outhouse roof, gazing wide-eyed down at the bubbles, and loudly inviting passers-by to come and see what they'd found. Father Adams, who was one of the people who did – years ago his grandfather had lived in the Westons' cottage and that, according to country politics, really gave him more right to walk up the front path than the Westons themselves, who were newcomers from town – said old man Weston turned all the colours of a shammylon when he saw he'd been found out. He hadn't been there long enough to know that practically everybody else – certainly Father Adams – filled their water-butts in exactly the same way, and for days he went round hardly daring to look anybody in the face. Which, as Aunt Ethel said the day Solomon ate her guinea pot of beauty cream, just showed the folly of having anything to do with Siamese at all.

We never managed to get the better of them ourselves. Every time we thought we had them weighed off, up they came with something new. Mouse-catching, for instance. No sooner had we got used to the routine of Sheba catching them and Solomon slinging them round our heads for hours than Sheba, feeling that Solomon was getting too much limelight, decided that she'd better tell us when she caught a mouse in future, so there would be no mistaking it was hers. The first time Solomon heard her coming under the new system, moaning like a travelling air-raid siren, he said it was ghosts and hid under the bath and we had an awful job to coax him out; but it wasn't long before he, in turn, thought up an even better gimmick. He ate the mouse. Not quietly, in a corner, but noisily on the hearthrug, leaving us the head and tail as souvenirs. The next thing was that Sheba ate a mouse too, but her stomach wasn't as strong as Solomon's and she went straight out and sicked it up on the stairs. And so, as Charles said, life went on.

There was a period, just after Sugieh died and the kittens were beginning to feel their feet as individuals, when if we had visitors we just couldn't move for them, sitting solidly in people's laps, licking their iced cakes when they weren't looking, investigating their handbags and chatting to them under the bathroom door. They liked people so much that when we shut them in the hall one night because one of Charles's friends had a dark suit on and wasn't very fond of cats anyway they climbed the curtains, got out through a transom window which we didn't know was open, and appeared suddenly with their small smudgy faces pressed to the window of the sitting room, gazing wistfully in like orphans of the storm.

A great success that was. Everybody cooed over them and gave them ice-cream and Charles's friend went home with a suit that looked as if it were made of angora. The next time they were shut out on account of visitors Solomon, remembering the ice-cream, promptly jumped out of a window again. This time, however, as all the hall windows were shut, old Bat Brains went upstairs and jumped out of the bedroom window. One visitor fainted on the spot when she saw him coming down, but he landed in a hydrangea and was quite unharmed. The only thing was that now Solomon had discovered that he could open windows by putting his fat little bullet-head under the catches and pushing them up, in addition to spreading twelve copies of *The Times* on the stairs any time we shut them out, we now had to tie up all the window catches with string as well.

Though the cats drove visitors nearly mad with their attentions when they first arrived, however, if anybody stayed after eleven o'clock things were very different. Then, retiring to the most comfortable armchair (if anybody was sitting in it they just squeezed down behind him and kept turning round and round till he got out; it never failed), they curled up and ostentatiously tried to go to sleep. Tried was the operative word. Any time anybody looked across at the chair there would be at least one Siamese regarding them with half-raised head, one eye open and a pained expression that clearly indicated it was time they went home, Some People were tired. If this had no effect, in due course Solomon would sit up, yawn noisily, and subside again with a loud sigh on top of Sheba. Few visitors missed that hint. Solomon yawned like fat men belch – long, loudly and with gusto. What was most embarrassing, though, was the way – after lying for hours as if they'd been working all day in a chain gang – they suddenly perked up the moment people did start to go. It wouldn't have been so bad if they'd just politely seen them off at the door, the way Sugieh used to do. These two sat in the hall and bawled to people to hurry up – and as we shepherded people to the front gate they could be seen quite plainly through the window, hilariously chasing one another over the chairs by way of celebration.

To be quite honest, by that time the visitors usually weren't looking with such a kindly eye on the cats either. There was the friend, for instance, who brought an old pair of stockings for playing with the cats and left her best ones in our bedroom for safety. She expected the old ones to be ruined, and she was right. Solomon gave her a friendly nip in the ankle while we were having tea and bang they went. Unfortunately the bedroom door wasn't properly shut and while Sheba was, of her own accord, bringing the new ones down for the lady they went bang too, hitched up in a snag on the stairs.

There was the friend who unthinkingly left her car keys on the hall table. An innocent enough gesture – except that

that was the time when Solomon was being an Alsatian dog and carrying things round in his mouth and it took us two hours to find where he had put them. Down the clock golf hole in the lawn.

There was the cactus which disappeared mysteriously from its pot while its owner, who had just been given it by another friend, was calling on us for a cup of tea. Charles said if that didn't prove Solomon wasn't right in the head nothing did – but as a matter of fact it wasn't Solomon. It was Sheba, as we discovered later when we started raising cactus ourselves and had to lock them in the bathroom every night for safety while she howled under the door for just a little one to play marbles with.

It was Solomon though, alone and unaided, who killed the fur coat. We laughed at the look of awe on his face the first time he saw it, and the way he immediately put up his back and offered to fight. We didn't give it a thought as the owner, patting him on the head and saying it was only a coat little man, tossed it nonchalantly on to the hall chair. But Solomon did. As soon as he'd had his share of the crab sandwiches he went out and killed it so dead I shudder even now to think how much it cost us to have it repaired.

We kept a strong guard on fur coats after that. Whenever one arrived Charles held Solomon in the kitchen while I personally locked it in the wardrobe and then locked the bedroom door. Even so I had qualms the night someone arrived wearing a particularly fine leopard coat and Solomon, as soon as supper was over, disappeared quietly into the hall. As soon as I could I slipped out too, to check. Everything seemed all right. The bedroom door was still firmly locked and when I spoke to him Solomon, sitting innocently on the hall table and gazing out into the night, said he was only looking for foxes.

It wasn't until the visitor, getting ready to go, started looking round the hall saying it was funny but she could have *sworn* she left it on the chest that I realized I hadn't taken her hat up to the bedroom as well – and by that time it was too late. It had – or rather it had had – a smart black cocksfeather cockade on one side. When we picked it up, from under the same chair that had once concealed Aunt Ethel's famous telegram, all the feathers fell off.

THIRTEEN

Sheik Solomon

By the time Solomon was six months old he had, despite his unpromising beginnings, grown into one of the most handsome Siamese we had ever seen. True he still had spotted whiskers and big feet and walked like Charlie Chaplin. But he had lost his puppy fat and was as lithe and sleek as a panther. His black, triangular mask – except for one solitary white hair right in the middle which he said he'd got through worrying over Sheba – shone like polished ebony. His eyes, set slantwise above high, Oriental cheekbones, were a brilliant sapphire and remarkable even for a Siamese. When he lay on the garden wall with his long black legs drooping elegantly over the edge he looked, according to Father Adams, exactly like a sheik in one of them Eastern palaces.

Father Adams, who was a great fan of Ethel M. Dell's, would have liked Solomon to be a sheik in the real romantic sense of the word. At that time he was still dreaming of making a fortune from cat-breeding and Solomon was so magnificent that there was nothing he would have liked more than to see him drag Mimi off into the hills by the scruff of her sleek cream neck and there found a race of Siamese that would, as he was always telling us, fetch ten quid apiece as easy as pie.

He was so disgusted when we had Solomon neutered that he wouldn't speak to us for a week – which was all very well; we didn't want to spoil Solomon's life either, but we had to share it with him and even our best friends wouldn't have lasted long in a house with an unneutered Siamese. The only way we could have kept him – unless we let him wander, in which case a Siamese tom usually develops into a terrible fighter and rarely comes home at all – would have been outside in a stud house.

When we asked Solomon about it he said he'd rather have beetles than girls. And cream cakes, he added, casting a speculative eye at the tea trolley. And sleeping in our bed, he said that night, burrowing determinedly under the blankets to find my head.

That settled it. We could as soon imagine Solomon a stud tom as pretending to be a lion at the zoo. The following weekend he was neutered, and Sheba along with him, and not a scrap of trouble did we have with either of them except in the matter of Sheba's stitches. Two she had, and the vet who did the operation – a town one this time; not for one moment did we attach any blame to the vet who did Sugieh's operation, but it seemed fairer all round to have Sheba done by someone else – said we could easily take them out ourselves on the tenth day. Just snip here and here, he said, pull smartly – and the job was done.

It might have been with normal cats, but not with Sheba. She wasn't going to have any ham-fisted amateurs handling her, she said. Every time we approached her with the scissors she fled to the top shelf of the bookcase and barricaded herself in. Even Charles couldn't get her to come down. She liked him very much, she assured him from behind the Britannicas – but not her stitches, if he didn't mind. He could practise on Solomon, Mimi or even me. She wanted a real doctor. After the night when the stitches began to itch and she lay on our bed first trying to get them out herself and then letting Solomon have a go until the perpetual snick-snicking nearly drove us mad she got one, too. We could hardly ask the local vet to do the job, as he hadn't done the operation, so the next morning we rang Doctor Tucker, who came over and obliged at once. Sheba didn't run away from him. She told him at great length what we'd tried to do to her and did he think he ought to report it to the Medical Association. Then, while he snipped and pulled with the self-same scissors we had tried to use, she stood quietly on the table, her eyes happily crossed, and purred.

That, we thought, was the end of our troubles. The cats were growing up now. They had their little idiosyncrasies of course. Like Sheba's habit of turning out the vegetable rack every night, followed by complaints from our new help that it wasn't her job in other houses to fish sprouts and squashed tomatoes from under the cooker every morning. Not that it mattered much because she gave us notice quite soon anyway on account of Solomon's habit of walking over floors as soon as she'd scrubbed them.

Sheba was jolly pleased when she went. Now, she said – and how right she was – she'd be able to file sprouts under the stove until they smelled real high before anybody moved them. Solomon was pleased. She kept throwing the floorcloth at him, he said, and if he hadn't been a gentleman – in the highest sense of the word, he said, ignoring Sheba's aside to Charles that he Wasn't Any More Was He, Not Since His Operation? – he'd have bitten her. Charles was pleased. If she hadn't gone, he said, judging by the looks she gave him when he asked her to empty the ash-trays she'd have been throwing the floorcloth at him next. The only one who wasn't pleased was me – and I was too busy doing the housework to complain.

There was Solomon's keen interest in things mechanical which led him to follow the vacuum cleaner like a bloodhound, with his nose glued firmly to the carpet, watching the bits disappear inside. Come to think of it, it was a good thing the help wasn't around the day he decided to experiment with that and, while I was moving a chair, poked his ball of silver paper curiously into the works. I turned round just in time to see a long black paw disappearing under the front and to hurl myself at the switch like a bomb.

Mrs Terry wouldn't have done that. She'd have screamed, thrown her apron over her head and fainted, the way she did when she removed the guard from the electric fire in the sitting room for cleaning and Solomon, with happy memories of Mum, promptly walked over and stuck his rear against it. The only result of that incident had been that for a while Solomon's tail, indented in two places by the electric bars, had looked more like that of a poodle than a Siamese and Sheba had made him cross by pretending to be frightened every time she saw it. What might have happened with the vacuum I hardly dared to think.

These though, as I have said, were idiosyncrasies such as all Siamese owners experience. So long as we got up at five in the morning to let them out – otherwise Sheba knocked the lamp off the dressing-table and Solomon bit us; so long as we only ate chocolates wrapped in silver paper and let Solomon have every single piece – he sulked like mad when somebody gave us a four-pound box for Christmas without an inch of silver paper among them: Done It On Purpose he said they had, watching disconsolately every time the box was opened, and couldn't we eat them faster than that; so long as we kept a box of All Bran permanently on the kitchen floor to fill the corners when he felt peckish – if we didn't he was liable to get in the cupboard and look for it himself with disastrous results; so long as we remembered little things like that we had no trouble at all. Real little home birds they were. Always running in to see that we hadn't gone for a walk without them – or even more important, that we weren't eating something behind their backs.

Which made it all the more worrying the morning I called the cats and instead of the usual mad stampede to see what was for breakfast only Sheba appeared, looking very small and forlorn and nattering anxiously that Solomon had vanished: she'd looked all over the place for him and she didn't know where he could be.

We didn't know it then but Solomon, tired of the chains of civilization, had gone to be an explorer – and, as explorers sometimes do, he had met with a hazard. When I found him an hour later, after scouring the countryside till I was practically on my knees, he was in a field more than a mile away with a pair of large and angry geese. When I panted up he was crouching in a corner bawling his head off about what he'd do if they came any nearer, but he didn't fool them – or me. He was scared stiff. His ears stuck up like a pair of horrified exclamation marks. His eyes were nearly popping out of his head. When I called him he gave a long, despairing wail which clearly signified that if I didn't hurry up the cannibals would get him, and he wasn't half in a fix.

I got him out of that by wading knee-deep in a bed of stinging nettles, leaning over a barbed wire fence and hauling him out by the scruff of his neck. From the look on the faces of those geese it was obvious there wasn't time to go round by the gate. He never learned, of course. No sooner was he safely on my shoulder and the geese out of ear-shot than the old bounce was back. All the way home I had a monologue right in my ear about what they said to him and what he said back – punctuated half-way by a decision, which I nipped in the bud by grabbing his tail and hanging on to it firmly, to go right back and tell them some more.

By the time we got home Solomon, in his own mind at least, was a budding Marco Polo. And from then on we had hardly a moment's peace. Summoned by a wail that turned my blood cold when I heard it, I rescued him from one emergency after another. Once, under the impression that she was running away from *him*, he chased a cow that was being tormented by flies. That was fine fun while it lasted, tearing across the field with the wind in his tail and his long black legs going like a racehorse – until the cow turned round, saw Buffalo Bill capering cockily at her heels, and chased him instead.

I rescued him that time from a handy wall, doing a fine imitation of the Stag at Bay with the cow's horns about an inch from his trembling black nose. The time he frightened a little lamb, though, he wasn't so lucky. His nearest point of escape then was through a hedge which topped a steep bank above the woods, and by the time he made it the lamb's mother was so close behind he couldn't stop to look for a proper way through. As I toiled wearily up through the woods in answer to his yell for help he appeared dramatically on the skyline, leapt into space, and landed ignominiously in a pool of mud.

That taught him nothing either. The very next day I saw him – in his own inimitable way, which meant laboriously hiding behind every blade of grass he came across and crawling across the open bits on his stomach – tracking a small kitten into the self-same woods. I let him go that time. His dusky face was alight with eagerness, there was such an Excelsior light in his eyes – and he couldn't, I thought, get into trouble with a little kitten like that.

That was where I was wrong. A few minutes later there was a volcanic explosion, a mad crashing of branches, silence – and then, once more, the familiar sound of Solomon yelling for help. Creeping stealthily through the woods he had, it seemed, come across his enemy from the farmyard, doing a bit of mousing. Judging by the way the tom went streaking up the road as I dashed into the woods he was just as alarmed as Solomon by the encounter – and indeed it wasn't that that Columbus was belly-aching about. It was that just as he had taken refuge up a tree, so had the kitten. Up the same tree. Solomon had made it first and was clinging for dear life six feet up while the kitten, unable to pass him, was directly under his tail. Solomon, in all his glory, a magnificent, intimidating specimen of a male Siamese, was howling because a tiny kitten no bigger than a flea wouldn't let him get down.

After that Solomon kept away from the woods for a while. He took to sitting on the garden wall instead, pretending, when we asked him why he hadn't gone exploring, that he was Waiting for a Friend. That, unfortunately, was how he came to get interested in horses. Unfortunately – because when Solomon got interested in anything he invariably wanted a closer look. Unfortunately – because it wasn't long before the owner of the local riding school was ringing us up to ask whether we would mind keeping him in while her pupils went by. He was frightening the horses, she said. Little Patricia had already fallen into our stinging nettles twice, and her mother didn't like it.

When we said, somewhat indignantly, that cats didn't frighten horses, she said ours did. She said he lurked in the grass until the first one had gone by, then dashed out into the road and pranced along behind him. It looked, she said, almost as if he was imitating the horse – though that of course was ridiculous. The first horse was all right because he couldn't see the cat; the ones behind, she said – and we could quite see her point – nearly had hysterics.

We saw to it that after that Solomon did his imitations from the hall window when the riding school went by. Unfortunately, while it was easy enough to tell when they were coming – what with the trampling of hoofs and instructions to people to watch their knees or keep their eyes on their elbows they made, according to Father Adams, more noise than the ruddy Campbells – solitary riders were different. Sometimes we were in time to stop Trigger the Second following his latest idol down the lane. More often the first we knew that a horse had passed that way was when once again Solomon was missing.

It was very worrying. Sometimes it would be a couple of hours or more before he came plodding back on his long thin legs, looking rather sheepish and trying to slip through the gate so that he could pretend he'd been there all the time. We tried everything we could think of, short of a cage, to curb this latest craze. We even bought some goldfish, seeing it was things that moved he liked, and set up a special tank for him in the sitting room.

Sheba and Charles thought they were wonderful. They sat in front of the tank for ages goggling like a couple of tennis fans as the fish flipped and glided lazily through the water. Solomon, however, when he found there was no way in at the top or sides and that they didn't run away when he looked at them, lost interest and slipped silently out. Charles was too intent on the fish to see him go, or to notice the lone, red-coated rider clopping up the lane; and I was in the kitchen. The first I knew of his latest escapade was when the 'phone rang and a farmer from the other end of the valley said he didn't know whether I knew it but that black-faced cat of ours had just gone by following one of the huntsmen. He was going it well, he said, stepping it out like a proper little Arab. But the horse was a kicker with a red ribbon on its tail and he didn't…

I didn't wait to hear any more. I dropped the 'phone and ran. When I caught up with them Solomon was still, unknown to the rider, following doggedly along behind that pair of wicked-looking hoofs. The huntsman stared in admiration as I picked him up. Plucky little devil, he said, to have followed all that way. Ought to have been a horse himself.

He didn't know me, of course, or Solomon from Adam. He looked a little alarmed when, holding old Bat Ears firmly by the scruff of his neck, I said it was a remark like that which started all this horse business in the first place.

FOURTEEN

The Great Pheasant Mystery

There was a time when our garden was practically a naturalist's paradise. Jackdaws nested in our chimney. If during the breeding season we never got a wink of sleep after daybreak, what with first the parents getting up and talking to one another and later on four or five youngsters hissing non-stop for breakfast only a brick's width from our ears – what, as Charles said, was that compared with the sight of a black feathered rear sticking trustfully out of our chimney pot while its owner fed the offspring underneath?

Thrushes, bursting with confidence, banged their snails on our path till it sounded like a blacksmith's and looked like a cockle-stall at Southend. Blackbirds, joining us for meals on the lawn and heaving worms out of the ground like lengths of elastic, put more visitors off their food than we could count.

One year – just, according to my grandmother, to show how Mother Nature trusted us – we even had a baby cuckoo on our doorstep. Every morning when I opened the front door it was squatting on the porch, close up to the milk-bottle. We never knew why – unless it was lonely and thought the bottle was another cuckoo. It never attempted to get at the milk and as soon as I brought the bottle indoors it flapped and fluttered round to the back where it sat all day on a heap of stones, watching us stolidly through the kitchen window.

Even when it was being fed by a depressed-looking hedge-sparrow that soon had to hover in mid-air to get anywhere near that cavernous mouth it still watched us. We were jolly glad when it grew up and went off to Africa. My grandmother, bitterly disappointed because we wouldn't let her rear it at home – it reminded her of Gladstone, she said, and Aunt Louisa could easily have fed it – said we didn't deserve the trust of innocent little creatures. Charles said innocent little creatures be blowed – the way that damned thing had watched his every move for weeks he felt so furtive he expected to be arrested by Scotland Yard every time he set foot outside the door.

It was interesting all the same. What with the cuckoo, the robin that used to come in and perch on a chair while we ate and the woodpecker that went a bit queer in the head and started pecking a hole in a nearby telegraph pole in the middle of winter – we watched that entranced for days until somebody told the Post Office about it and they came out and tacked a metal plate over the hole – we saw ourselves as budding Ludwig Kochs. And then we had the cats.

After that the sensible birds gave the cottage a wide berth. Any time they had to fly over our territory when the cats were about they zoomed smartly up at the front gate and flew over at ceiling height until they reached the back. The jackdaws persevered for a while but even they gave up when Sheba climbed the chimney stack one day and looked meaningly at them through the cowl. The only bird that came near us when the cats were about – and he disappeared pretty smartly when Sheba looked round the corner – was the blackbird who used to play with Solomon. At least the blackbird was playing, as birds sometimes do – flying low over Solly's head as he crossed the lawn, uttering mocking little cries and perching enticingly on the wall. Solly wasn't. He went after him like a Wimbledon champion, leaping spectacularly through the air with his paws going in all directions.

That, actually, was where the blackbird made his mistake. He had obviously watched Solomon hunting mice in the garden and summed him up as a blockhead who couldn't catch anything. He hadn't seen him indoors, practising with ping-pong balls and flies. Solomon with a ping-pong ball was a joy to watch. Sheba had what Charles loftily described as a typically female way of trying to catch things. When we threw a ball in the air for her she leapt hazily towards it, waved her paws and missed. It was surprising when you considered her prowess with mice – no less surprising than the fact that Solomon, who couldn't catch anything on the ground to save his life, could shoot through the air like an arrow and field anything we threw between his front paws while still in flight.

It was his only talent and he made the most of it. When we wouldn't throw balls for him, or rolled-up silver paper, he went round swatting flies. It was a little disturbing to have a cat continually sailing through the air as if he were Anton Dolin, particularly since he invariably came down again like a bomb, but it got rid of the flies. It also – though the blackbird didn't know it then – made it rather dangerous for little birds to make fun of him. One day, after a particularly good practice with a meat-fly, Solomon went out, leapt smartly into the air, and fielded two feathers out of old Smart-Alec's tail.

We knew the blackbird got away. We saw him with our own eyes, streaking down the valley as if the spooks were after him. Not, however, according to Solomon. He spent the rest of the evening swaggering round the place in a style we knew only too well – Charles called it Podgebelly's panther walk – with his head down, two black feathers sticking out of the corner of his mouth and a look which inferred that if you wanted to know where the rest of the bird was, he had it inside.

When he went to bed that night and the owls began to hoot across in the woods he got up and stalked to the window. There was a time, when he was a kitten, when he was scared of the owls and used to back rapidly under the bedclothes when they started up, but not now. Face pressed to the glass, his camel-like rear hunched threateningly in the air, he told them exactly what he'd do to *them* if they didn't shut up. Eat them and put their tails with the blackbird's.

Often in the days that followed I remembered Aunt Ethel's prediction that Solomon would grow up not quite right in the head. Watching him leaping round the lawn, shadow-boxing – on the strength of two blackbird's feathers – everything that flew over from a sparrow to an aeroplane, I wondered which of us would end up in a strait-jacket first. Solomon or me.

When he went out of the door now it was on his stomach, in case there was one round the corner. When he patrolled the garden – with reproving glances at the potting shed where Sheba, he said, made far too much noise talking to Sidney and frightened them away – it was with the narrowed eye and stealthy tread of the hunter. When he slept before the fire, stomach up to catch the heat, it was no longer the deep, tranquil sleep of somebody with nothing but crab sandwiches on his mind; he caught dream birds so energetically it looked as if he had St Vitus's dance.

They were the only birds he did catch. No live ones ever came within swatting distance again. To make up for it, if there was a dead bird lying around within a mile radius, Solomon brought that home instead.

Sometimes it was very dead – like the crow that must have been shot quite a month before and nearly fell to pieces when Solomon laid it triumphantly on the carpet. We picked that up in a shovel and returned it hurriedly to the woods – better make sure it was off our premises, said Charles; we didn't want anybody thinking Solomon had killed it. Actually I thought Charles was being a bit over-cautious there. Even Solomon's greatest admirer could hardly have believed him capable of shooting a crow with a twelve-bore shot gun. But I said nothing. It didn't make much difference anyway. The next day the crow was back again.

By A Great Stroke of Luck, said Solomon, laying it lovingly on the carpet where it positively vibrated with age, he had gone another way through the woods than was his wont, and there it was under some leaves. Nice, wasn't it? he demanded, licking a limp-looking feather carefully into place and settling down possessively beside it. Almost as good as new. He was going to Keep It For Ever and Ever, he added loudly, looking round to make sure that Charles was listening. But Charles, holding his nose, had already gone for the disinfectant.

After that Charles listened to me and Solomon's trophies went in the dustbin, with the lid hammered on so that he couldn't get them out again. He tried hard enough. He practically did a skiffle act all on his own, scratching frantically at the lid and wailing loudly for his fowl's head he'd discovered on Father Adams's rubbish heap and his pigeon's wing that he'd found up the lane.

Charles said if the crow had been dead a month, the pigeon must have died during the Roman occupation – but smell didn't worry Solomon. The more it reeked, the more ghastly the specimen looked, the better he was pleased. So long, that was, as he had found it himself. If *we* gave him something that wasn't perfectly fresh – meat bought one day, for instance, and offered to him for supper on the next – he stared at us in horror and said surely we didn't expect him to eat That. Sheba was just as bad. Trying to Poison Us, she would wail, reeling dramatically back at the first unbelieving sniff. After which they would go and sit forlornly side by side on the garden wall, asking passers-by in sad, small voices whether they had any spare food on them, or knew of a good home for two little cats that nobody wanted.

Weekends were the worst. Often by the time we got to Sunday night I was at my wits' end over feeding those animals. I might buy two pounds or more of perfectly fresh meat on Friday – and by Saturday lunchtime, if it was a warm day, they refused to touch it. Fish was out for the same reason. They wouldn't even eat that for Saturday breakfast. Tinned cat food set their ears on edge with horror. Siamese never ate *that*, they announced. Not even in an emergency. Best tinned beef or veal was acceptable for one meal. After that, that too was out. Siamese, they said, marching sadly out to the wall in dignified procession, needed Variety.

Week after week Sheba, looking so fragile it practically brought tears to my eyes, even though I knew she was putting it on, ate nothing at all on Sundays, while Solomon existed ostentatiously on All Bran. Our hearts sank every time we saw the open cupboard and the tell-tale packet on the floor with the hole hungrily torn in its side – mute reminders of the fact that we Weren't Feeding Them Properly. Wistfully we remembered Blondin – happy as a king with a couple of nuts and a slice of orange... his only vices a passion for trouser buttons and a tendency to stick his tongue hopefully down the spout of the teapot when nobody was looking... With a sigh of regret for the past we went out and ordered a refrigerator.

The day it arrived, a bright, gleaming symbol of their victory in the fight for fresher food for Siamese, Solomon – sometimes it seemed there was no *end* to the trouble that cat could cook up for us – brought home his biggest trophy yet. Irving himself couldn't have devised a more effective entrance. The men on their knees in the kitchen fixing the wires; myself making a friendly cup of tea; Sheba sitting, wide-eyed and inquisitive, right in front as usual and one of the men asking her jocularly whether she thought it was going to be big enough to keep her mice in; Charles working out how many bottles of beer it would hold – and suddenly Solomon, his eyes shining like stars above a cloud of feathers, his long thin legs spread wide to avoid the trailing wings, staggering in with a big cock-pheasant.

You could have cut the silence with a knife as he laid it at my feet and cuffed a stray feather off his nose. The men looked at one another under the peaks of their caps. We knew what they were thinking – that they'd happened on a neat little poaching set-up where we used Siamese cats instead of dogs and, poachers being what they were, the sooner they happened out of it again the better.

Charles tried hard to mend matters by explaining about Solomon's habit of bringing dead things home from the woods. Giving the body a nonchalant push with his foot he said Ha! Ha! Like the old crow he brought home he supposed – fell to pieces the moment you touched it. This one didn't fall to pieces. It rolled over with a solid, healthy thud, whereupon Solomon leapt at it with a fiendish yell and warned it to get up again if it dared. The men, scared out of their wits, finished as hurriedly as they could and fled. They hardly spoke another word to us, but as their van leapt away up the lane a hushed voice floated out through the window. No wonder they wanted a refrigerator, it said.

One thing we did know. Wherever Solomon had got the pheasant he hadn't caught it himself. A blackbird's tail-feathers were one thing – but a bird that size would only have had to flap its wings at him and he'd have been up the nearest tree screaming for the fire brigade.

He might have stolen it from somebody's larder. It was equally possible that one of the local game-keepers had dropped it over the gate as a present in passing, as country people, shy of receiving thanks, sometimes do – and that Solomon had simply picked it up and brought it in.

We never knew the answer. For two days it lay hidden under the bath with Solomon trying to batter the door down and Charles alternately saying that it seemed a shame to waste it and that men had been sent to Botany Bay for less. We hoped somebody might drop a clue as to where it had come from, but they didn't. If it had come out of somebody's larder it was, as Charles said, quite obvious that it hadn't got there legitimately either. We dared not make enquiries for fear, if it wasn't a present, of branding Solomon as a poacher. Having spent every waking moment since the day he was born trying to impress people with his toughness it was, after all, only natural for them to believe him.

On the second night therefore – since, quite apart from conscience, we could hardly eat a bird which might (if one followed another line of thought) have died from poisoning, we crept out after dark with the body wrapped in a bag, walked two miles into the hills, and regretfully buried it in a ditch.

FIFTEEN

Solomon's Romance

How nice, people said – watching them march in majestic procession up the garden trouble-bent for Charles's latest batch of cabbage plants, or posed lovingly cheek to cheek in an armchair like a picture on a Christmas card – to have two Siamese cats.

In some ways it was. They were company for each other when we were out – and where, as Solomon said himself, could he have put his head when he slept in front of the fire on winter nights, if it wasn't for Sheba's stomach?

On the debit side, however, the mischief those two led each other into outdid a cage of monkeys. The time Sheba stowed away in Sidney's side-car for instance, and he didn't find her until he got home and then had to turn round and bring her all the way back – she'd never have thought of

137

that on her own. Sheba was a home girl. She rarely went far from the garden herself and any time Solomon went off on one of his jaunts she could be depended on, to his disgust, to be standing gleefully in the porch bawling here he was and were we going to smack his bottom now as he tried to sidle surreptitiously up the path.

He could boast as much as he liked about where he'd been and what he'd done. Sheba wasn't interested. She preferred to stay at home and be Charles's and Sidney's little friend. Until she heard Solomon yelling one day to look where he was now – and when she did, there he was out in the lane sitting on the bonnet of a stationary car. She took one look at him, started to shout for Charles, and changed her mind. She had been good for so long that life had, to tell the truth, become rather boring. Besides, however often she advised it, Solomon never did get his bottom smacked. Instead he was made so much fuss of when he did come back from his wanderings that her prissy little nose was put rather out of joint... Without more ado she joined him on the bonnet of the car.

After that the moment anybody parked a car outside the cottage the pair of them were gone like a flash. To begin with they just sat on the front chatting madly to passers-by. That was bad enough. I nearly wore myself to a shadow rushing out to shoo them off and wipe away the paw marks before the owner returned. Then Solomon discovered that a car has an inside. I remember perfectly the day he found that out. Rushing out to grab them off the bonnet of a big black Humber, polishing away busily at the paw marks as I did so, I suddenly realized that he was staring incredulously at something through the windscreen, and when I looked to see what it was there was an old lady sitting in the back seat, staring equally incredulously back. Grinning weakly – it was all I could think of *to* do – I grabbed the cats and fled. It was pointless, of course. Solomon, having spotted the old lady, was determined to have a closer look. The moment I put him down on the lawn he was away over the wall again like a shot, this time clinging firmly to the door handle with both paws while he peered intently through the window.

Solomon, when he is determined, has claws like grappling hooks. I just couldn't get them off the door handle, and what with him bawling with rage because he wanted to see the lady, Sheba in her usual strategic position up the damson tree advising me to smack him this time anyway and the old lady practically in a state of collapse thinking she was being attacked by a mad woman and an equally mad cat, I could think of only one thing to do. Holding Solomon firmly round the middle I yelled as hard as I could for Charles. Charles disentangled Solomon. Charles, while I carried Solomon into the house, pacified the old lady. It was a bit difficult, he said – she kept saying that when her son came back from his walk we would hear more of this – until he mentioned that I was his wife. Whereupon, he said – rather puzzled, because he didn't know yet about me rushing out and polishing the bonnet of her car while she was still inside it – she patted his hand, saying poor, poor boy, we all had our troubles and must bear them bravely, and gave him a peppermint.

I swore I'd never get Solomon off a car again. I did of course. I was always dragging him off, from under – and now, if ever he found an open window – from inside other people's cars. Charles wouldn't, so I had to. I dared not open the door, even if it wasn't locked. Charles said people might think we had nefarious intentions. So there, sometimes two and three times a day, I stood dangling a long piece of string through the windows of strange cars, frantically imploring Solomon to be a good cat and come out before the owners returned. I held the string at arm's length and stood as far back from the car as I could. Nobody could possibly have thought I had nefarious intentions, but quite a few must have thought I had a screw loose. Particularly since Solomon never paid any attention anyway, but either lay at full length along the top of the back seat pretending to passers-by that it was All His and he was Waiting for the Driver or else was quite invisible on the floor, nosing around among the parcels.

He knew he was doing wrong. He always nipped smartly out again a split second before the owner returned. But I was terribly afraid that one day he – and I – would be caught. I was afraid, too, that one day he might get in a car without my knowing it and be driven off without the driver knowing it either. Automatically I dropped whatever I was doing and rushed to the front gate every time I heard a car. Then in the end, of course, as I might have expected if I'd stopped to consider how those cats' minds worked, it wasn't Solomon who got carried off, but Sheba.

Far more cautious than her brother, she never risked getting inside a car herself. The most she would do, while I fished frantically for him with a piece of string, was to sit wide-eyed on the bonnet saying he was naughty, wasn't he, and she didn't know what we were going to do with him. She was longing to try it herself all the same. You could see it written all over her small blue face. So when at last the impulse became too great for her she went, obviously reasoning that she knew Sidney and would be quite safe with him, and sat in his side-car – and, such is the injustice of the world, promptly got abducted for her pains.

Solomon was beside himself with glee when she came back. This time it was his turn to do the shouting, and he made the most of it. Here she was, the Cross-Eyed Wonder Herself, he yelled stalking to meet her as she came, looking rather sheepish, down the path in Sidney's arms. What About Us Smacking Her Bottom For a Change, he roared in a voice that would have done credit to a lighthouse-keeper. He didn't wait for an answer. As soon as Sidney put her down he bowled her over himself, just to show who was who.

Usually, of course, it was the other way round. Sheba did the preliminary explorations and Solomon followed them up and got into trouble. The hole at the top of the stairs, for instance, where the electricity wires went through from the new part of the cottage to the old – Charles had pasted a piece of paper over that and painted it, to camouflage the spot until he had time to fill it in properly. It was Sheba who discovered that there was a gap at the bottom of the paper with an intriguing draught blowing through it – but while she was content merely to squint underneath it was Solomon, bustling up all bluff and bluster, who promptly thrust his paw clean through it, warning whoever was in there that they'd better come out quick or he'd be in after them. What was more he liked the dramatic effect so much that every time it was papered in future he did it again, and whenever I took visitors upstairs I had to explain not only the large hole perpetually edged with torn paper, but why there was usually a large, goofy-looking Siamese shouting threats down it as well.

When we had new ceiling-height cupboards built in the kitchen it was Sheba who first ventured cautiously on to the draining board and opened a door with a small, inquisitive paw – but it was Solomon, once she had proved there was nothing there to hurt little cats, who banged them lustily open every day as part of the general routine. When we took them for a walk past the cornfield it was Sheba who first thought of livening things up by jumping on an occasional post and imploring Charles to lift her down – but it was Solomon who had to thunder up and down *every* one like a circus pony and finally, wild with excitement, jumped off on the wrong side and got lost in the corn.

Whatever was happening, Solomon had to be most important and the only one in the limelight – except when it came to something like having his ears cleaned or his coat combed. Then there never was a cat more willing that Sheba should be first. He sat by with great interest while we worked on her, sniffing at the cotton wool and the saucer of oil, peering knowledgeably into her ears and assuring us that they were absolutely filthy and she couldn't have washed them for *months*. The moment his turn arrived, however, Solomon was gone. Yelling that we were making a big mistake, he wasn't our cat at all, he dashed desperately from cover to cover, anchoring himself by his claws to the backs of chairs and the edges of carpets. And when at last the deed was done – two little screws of wool turned gently in his ears and a comb passed swiftly through his coat, though, as Father Adams said, from the howls it sounded as if we were sawing the legs off a herd of elephants – he went around with his ears turned sorrowfully down, gazing at us so reproachfully from underneath them that we hated ourselves for hours.

When the winter came and Sheba, treading gingerly out into the first snow they had ever seen, proved that it was quite safe to venture out it was Solomon who every night scratched and rattled at the door, demanding to be let out on the lawn where he tore flamboyantly round in a foot of snow with his tail stuck up like a periscope while she, having done a prim little patrol up the path and back, sat genteelly on the porch cleaning off her paws. In the same way, while it was Sheba who said that winter was a good time for catching birds because we fed them and took to sitting under the lilac every morning with her eyes fixed like sapphire moons on the temporary bird-table, it was Solomon who insisted on sitting hopefully on the table itself. Spoiling everything, Sheba wailed when we fetched them in so that the birds could feed in peace, though Solomon insisted that he was disguised as a piece of bread.

There were some things, however, in which they were unanimous. Like not coming in when we called them and not wanting anybody else to live with us. They got quite worried about that at one time. There was, living further down the lane, a pretty short-haired blue queen with amber eyes called Susie, whose one failing was that she loved everybody. She loved dogs, she loved humans, she loved other cats – she even loved the rangy, battle-scarred tom from the farm, as witnessed by the fact that of the squads of kittens she had every year at least nine-tenths were bull-headed and black and white. And one day, to his absolute horror, she fell in love with Solomon.

He tried looking at her. He explained loudly and at great length that he liked beetles better than girls. It was no good. Every time he put his head out of the door there was Susie sitting on the porch, purring like a sewing machine and waiting to rub cheeks. The expression on his face as he walked self-consciously up the garden pretending he didn't know she was tripping adoringly alongside him was priceless. So was the way, if he saw her coming first, he nipped indoors and peered apprehensively round the hall curtains till she'd gone. Eventually she got wise to that, started coming in to look for him, and, passing the feeding dishes on the way and reasoning romantically that Lover Boy would want her to share his jug of wine and loaf of bread like in the poem, took to polishing off the contents on the way.

She was wrong there. Lover Boy wouldn't even have given his grandmother a sniff at the dustbin if he could help it, while Sheba was so enraged she forgot all about being a lady, hid behind the door one day and, for the first time in her life, hit Susie on the nose as she passed.

It didn't help any that we liked Susie and made a fuss of her when she came. Encouraging her to eat his food, wailed Solomon, glowering darkly round the door from a position where he could dodge the moment she started looking lovingly in his direction. Inviting her into our house, complained Sheba, jealously watching her rub against Charles's leg. Why didn't we have her to live with us and have done with it, they demanded indignantly the day they found her washing herself placidly in front of the fire.

That, as a matter of fact, had occurred to Susie herself. The next time she came she brought along a half-grown black and white kitten. After we had put her outside and told her to go home – much as we liked Susie this really was too much of a good thing – she took the kitten into the coalhouse and slept there all night on the paper sack. It wasn't that she didn't have a home to go to. It was just, she purred happily, shepherding her offspring through the back door at seven the next morning in the direction of the feeding dishes, that she loved Solly, and our cooking, so much she had decided to live with us instead.

We spent that day in a state of siege, with the back door firmly shut against the invaders and our two telling them to go home from every window in turn. Eventually it began to rain, and to our relief they went – though we felt terribly mean as we watched the long thin blue rear and the little squat black and white one disappearing sadly down the lane.

Half an hour later, with the rain still coming down in sheets, we heard faint squeaks from outside the back door. We looked at each other in dismay. 'She's got that kitten out there again,' said Charles. 'It'll absolutely drown in all this rain!' Good thing too, said Solomon, lying on his stomach and trying to peer under the door. That might teach it not to eat his food. But the thought of that little shrimp sleeping on the coal all night, getting no breakfast and now shivering out there in the rain all because of Susie's love for Solomon, was too much for us. Defeated we opened the door – and our eyes nearly shot out on stalks.

There in the pouring rain sat not the little black and white waif of the night before, but two beautiful blue kittens with round topaz eyes, their mouths wide open in a tremolo wail. They had obviously been rehearsed. We had never seen them before, but the moment the door opened they raised two perky little tails and marched boldly in. As they did so Susie jumped off the kitchen windowsill, where she had been waiting, and prepared to follow them. They were the very best she had, she explained in her shrill little voice. As we obviously only liked superior cats, could she bring them to live with us instead? It was one of the hardest things I have ever done, saying that she couldn't, and shutting the door in their faces.

SIXTEEN

Three Years' Hard

It is three years now since Solomon and Sheba came into our lives. Sometimes – it is a symptom common among Siamese owners – it seems like thirty. In that time there have been divers changes in our household. We no longer have Shorty, for instance. He died quite suddenly last year. We felt so guilty in case it was the result of being perpetually knocked off his hook by Solomon and Sheba – though indeed, wedged securely in the armchair in his cage and swearing heartily away with a cat either side of him he always seemed quite to enjoy it – that we sent him to the Ministry of Agriculture for a post-mortem.

When the report came back a weight was lifted from all our consciences. He had, it said – though how he had managed it on birdseed and water was a mystery – died from a fatty heart and enlarged liver. We didn't replace him. With the cats around it didn't seem fair – and anyway his cage had hardly been relegated sadly to the woodshed for more than a week before Solomon, climbing inquisitively over a pile of junk, fell on it and reduced it to a shape which made it, as he himself said after carefully inspecting the damage, quite impossible to keep a little bird in again.

We still have the fish – though their lives too have not been without event. Last winter the biggest of the lot developed fungus on his head and gills. For a fortnight, while everybody heroically ate shop cake, he swam sadly round in a special fungus-clearing solution in the pastry bowl. At the end of that time the fungus was still gaining and it looked very much as if we might have to listen to Sheba, who visited him hopefully every day and, when she found she couldn't reach him on account of the cake rack tied over the top of the bowl, strongly advised us to hit him on the head and put him down the drain. In desperation I tried a remedy I found in a book in the public library. Put the fish in a solution of one teaspoonful of common salt to a quart of water, it said, increasing the quantity of salt by an additional teaspoonful each day for four days.

It didn't seem to do our fish much good. Indeed by the evening of the third day he was floating round the bowl on his side, practically at his last gasp. It was Charles who, in a sudden flash of inspiration, realized the truth – that on account of the damp weather the salt we had been using was much more concentrated than usual, and that in consequence we had practically pickled the little chap alive. In a twinkling we had him out of his brine bath and into a bowl of warm, clean water.

But still he floated. Overcome with remorse we sat up till midnight, taking it in turn to hold him upright and steer him round the bowl by his tail until, at long last, our efforts were rewarded and it gave a faint flicker of its own accord. He recovered rapidly and within a short time, the fungus completely cleared, we were able to return him to the tank. The odd thing was that whereas before he had been completely gold, where the salt had acted on the fungus he was now black. He had a black head and gills, black tips to his fins and a black tail. He looked – said Charles, roaring with laughter, much to the disgust of Solomon who knew he was being talked about and immediately put down his ears and sulked – exactly like old Podgebelly. There was another interesting thing. We had never known before whether our fish, swimming somnolently round in their tank, were male or female. They all behaved exactly the same. Not, however, after the salt bath. Within a few days Podgebelly's double, his smart black tail waggling rakishly through the water, was chasing the girls like mad.

Solomon and Sheba have had their ups and downs as well. Sheba, not long ago, was bitten on the tail by one of the local toms. How she – so coy she closed her eyes and practically swooned if you so much as glanced at her, so prim she always looked as if she were wearing mittens and a mob cap – could have let such a mangy specimen of feline manhood come within half a mile of her was a mystery, but even she, I suppose, has her romantic moments. She paid for that one, a week later, with an abscess as big as a tangerine on her tail. True to form she was very brave when we took her to the vet, allowing him to open the abscess and pump a penicillin injection into her rump with an air of fragile martyrdom that practically had him in tears over his hypodermic. He said we must keep the incision open for a week, draining it and inserting a penicillin tube twice a day. With some cats, he said, that could be the devil of a job, but with this little sweetheart – here Sheba closed her eyes and smirked at him; the way, no doubt, she had smirked at the tom before he bit her tail – we would obviously have no trouble at all.

That was what he thought. Sheba and a handsome young vet was one thing. Sheba and ourselves was quite another. *He* could open an inch and a half of her tail with a scalpel and all she did was languish at him. We only had to pick up the bottle of Dettol and she was streaking up the hill to the Rector's like a comet, yelling to hide her quick, we were going to torture her.

As if that weren't enough to put up with, Solomon met the same cat a day or two later in the lane, stalked up and stuck his neck out at him like an ostrich – instead of taking to his heels as any normal cat would have done – and promptly got slashed on the cheek. It was only a small cut – but doing Sheba's tail was a picnic to trying to see to that. She, after all, was very small and frail. If we could stop her getting out of the house we could, with Father Adams to help us, usually corner her somewhere and minister to her; even if it was flat on our stomachs under the table like a rugger scrum. But Solomon was so powerful even three of us couldn't hold him still. The cat book said the way to deal with an awkward cat was to clutch him by the scruff of the neck and press him firmly down on the table. But Solomon had so much scruff he could turn round inside it, with the remarkable result that while *we* were holding him by the back of the neck he was flat on his back waving his paws like a windmill. The only way we could cope with him was for me to drag him round and round the floor on my hands and knees pretending he was a kitten, and getting a dab in with the Dettol when I could.

They had, needless to say, fully recovered by the time the grandfather clock arrived. The man who came to set it up laughed when I asked about having it hooked to the wall so that they couldn't knock it over. No cats couldn't hurt that old beauty he said, affectionately patting its walnut sides. They'd made things to last when they made he.

They had indeed. That clock, which had come to us on the death of my grandmother's brother, had belonged to my great-great-grandfather, and what with his years in the family shipping business in New York and his son's sojourn as a sheep-farmer on the River Plate it had done some travelling in its time. 'Twice round the Horn and the scars to show it,' great-grandfather used to say, after nostalgia for good old English beer and a couple of Victorian policemen to push him home on a barrow at closing time had brought him home to final retirement in the land of his birth. The scars were still there. Deep chips out of its base where it had slipped its moorings once in a gale and fallen, as great-grandfather himself was always doing, over his sea-chest. Neither great-grandfather nor Cape Horn, however, had ever subjected that poor old clock to the indignities it suffered at the hands of those cats.

The man had no sooner hung the weights, set the pendulum with loving care and departed than they were on it like a gang of demolition workers. Sheba perched on top, sneezing indignantly because she had found a crack that hadn't been properly dusted, and Solomon – expert, from long practice with the pantry, at opening doors – with his head inside watching the works. It superseded all other interests. For a while even the joys of tearing up the stair carpet and sitting on cars were forgotten. When it struck they fell over one another in a mad dash to the hall in case the works were falling out. When I wound it up Sheba hung over the top dabbing at the hands while Solomon, with a triumphant howl, sprang up my back and stood on my head to join her.

I worried when the weights were up in case the clock was top heavy and Sheba, leaping like a spawning salmon from the hall chest, might tip it over. When they were down I was scared of Solomon, whom we usually saw these days as two spidery back legs and a long black tail hanging out of the clock case, getting tangled up in them and being dragged inside. I worried so much that when we went out I took no chances either with the clock or the cats. In addition to tying up the window catches and putting newspapers on the stairs I now tied a piece of rope round the clock case so that Solomon couldn't open it, and dragged a heavy armchair against it so that Sheba couldn't knock it over.

Eventually we found a key for the door and Charles screwed the clock itself to the wall. Not, however, before it had served as another example to the village of our being as mad as hatters. Usually the first thing I did when I got home was to restore the hall to normal, but one night, being particularly tired, I left it. That, naturally, was the night one of the village ladies called to leave a collecting envelope for charity. There was rather an odd look on her face when I explained the avalanche of newspapers at the bottom of the stairs, the rope tied rakishly round the clock and the armchair pushed hurriedly against its middle; particularly since at that moment the cats, busily eating their supper in the kitchen, were nowhere in sight. There was an even odder one when, half an hour later, she returned to pick up the envelope and saw that what I had said was true. One Siamese was squatting like a cross-eyed owl on top of the clock and the other, with his head inside it, was delivering a running commentary on the works.

Not that the village needed any extra confirmation of their belief that we are cuckoo. They have had quite enough evidence of that in the past three years. Myself on the mornings we have to be away early, for instance, charging up the lane in my dressing-gown carrying a cat basket and barking like a dog. I take the cat basket because it is quite impossible to carry two Siamese, squirming like demented eels, together; if and when I am lucky enough to catch up with them Sheba rides home in the basket and Solomon, wailing tearfully about this being The Morning he Wanted to Be A Horse, hangs down my back like a sack. I bark because it does – sometimes – deceive them into thinking there is a dog about and halts them in their tracks. I am in my dressing-gown because if I don't start out after them the moment they disappear, by the time I am dressed they are quite likely to be strolling happily through the next village.

It is no good explaining this to people, of course. They just think we are mad. Like the two early-morning walkers on whom I once, still in my dressing-gown, descended like Tarzan from the woods. I can see their faces now as I came slithering down the steep, muddy path, grabbing wildly at the passing branches to steady myself and finally, losing my balance, sliding the last few yards to the road on the seat of my pyjamas. I explained that I was looking for a Siamese cat. It didn't help matters at all that at that moment two Siamese cats came ambling elegantly out of the front gate enquiring in tones of pained surprise what on earth was I sitting in the road like that for; *they* had been waiting in the garden for hours.

It was the same when Sheba, balance-walking along the ridge of the cottage roof one day after it had been raining, slipped on a wet tile and lost her nerve. There was no audience for the half hour during which she sat terror stricken on the ridge bawling for Charles to save her and Solomon, apprehension in every line of his triangular black face, howled in sympathy on the lawn; nobody to help us when at last, convinced that she really was stuck, we heaved the long extending ladder up on to the hillside and from there across to the roof. No sooner had Charles crawled along it, however, and got himself equally stuck on the ridge than the valley was suddenly alive with onlookers. Father Adams on the way to the pub, the riding school out for morning exercise, and a detachment of boy scouts disembarking for a nature ramble from a bus on the corner. It was no good, either, trying to explain to any of them why he was up there. By that time Sheba had come down off the roof all by herself and was merrily chasing Solomon round the lawn.

One expects that sort of thing from Siamese, of course; but in time it tells. Three years ago I hadn't a white hair in my head. As for Charles – even as I have been writing this last chapter he has fallen downstairs again.

For all that we wouldn't be without them. It is as impossible to imagine the cottage now without Siamese cats as it once was without a squirrel. They are coming down the hill now as I write. Sheba marching in front, putting down her small blue paws with the precision of a WAAF sergeant-major; Solomon ambling along in the rear, stopping occasionally to sniff at a daisy or to look over his shoulder in case there should be something interesting behind, and then having to run on his long, spindly black legs to catch up. In a moment they will come tearing up the stairs to stand side by side in the doorway, gazing at me as suspiciously as if it were I, not they, who left the ball on the stairs for Charles to slip on. Long – even Charles, tenderly bathing his bumps in the bathroom, says he agrees with me – may they continue to do so.

Feline Philosophy
Life Lessons from your Cat

Mike Hatt

£4.99 Hardback

With priorities including grooming and chasing butterflies, cats know how to make the most of their nine lives. Our kitty companions understand what matters: a dish full of food, a clean litterbox, and a comfortable spot for no-stress meditation.

Paws and reflect – these purrls of wisdom will enrich every day, or at least encourage you to take more naps.

Cats
Quotes and Stuff

£4.99 Hardback

*'Thousands of years ago, cats were worshipped as gods.
Cats have never forgotten this'*

Bursting at the seams with quotes, poems, jokes and stories, this book is a delightful celebration of the world's favourite furry friend.

The purrfect gift for every cat-lover.

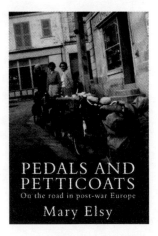

Pedals and Petticoats
On the Road in Post-war Europe

Mary Elsy

£7.99 Paperback

Christmas, 1950. Five years after D-Day, Britain was still recovering from the aftermath of war when four British girls – Mary Elsy, her sister Barbara and their friends Agnes and Esme – hatched a daring plan to give up their jobs and cycle through Europe. They would camp together in one tent on a shoestring budget, and ride 3,000 miles through battle-scarred Germany, France, Austria, Italy, Spain, Belgium and Luxembourg.

Although the Second World War was now firmly in the past, the ruins they found in Europe, especially in the Rhineland, were a sobering reminder of the destruction it had brought to both sides. At a time when few people were travelling for recreation, Mary Elsy's young all-female party created a stir everywhere they went.

With its fascinating cast of characters, *Pedals and Petticoats* is both a classic travel memoir and a charming eyewitness account of life in post-war Europe.

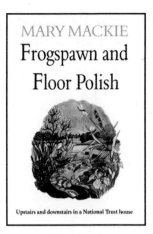

Frogspawn and Floor Polish

Upstairs and Downstairs in a
National Trust House

Mary Mackie

£6.99 Paperback

*'I've never forgotten the photographer who came in as white as a
sheet and said he hadn't realised the fence was electrified.
Until he was astride it. Nasty'*

Join Mary Mackie and husband Chris as they revisit
Felbrigg Hall, the stately home they lived and worked
in for several years. Behind the beauty of the gardens,
resplendent with apple blossom and wisteria, and
beyond the imposing majesty of the seventeenth-century
architecture, a constant battle is waged against dust and
dirt, fungus and beetle, over-zealous conservationists, and
floors on the brink of collapse…

www.summersdale.com